GREAT HUNTING ADVENTURES

Edition 2
Volume I

Henry E. Prante

© 2014

GREAT HUNTING ADVENTURES

Volume I
Edition 2

Henry E. Prante
Published by Hella Prante
Copyright © 2014 Hella Prante

ISBN-13:
978-1499314595

ISBN-10:
1499314590

All rights reserved. No part of this book may be reproduced or transmitted in any form by any means without permission from the publisher, except by a reviewer, who may quote brief passages in a review.

Beach House Graphics Ltd. of Surrey BC. has generously allowed the re-use of the graphics from the previous print version of Great Hunting Adventures to be used in these eBook publications. Your beautiful artwork is much appreciated. Thank you.

DEDICATION

You are missed so much, Dad! You are always in our hearts and not forgotten!

Our family has never been the same without you here. With much love from Marilyn, Raymond, Wayne, Caressa, Monica, Michael, Hella &, wife, Brigitte, along with all the family in Germany as well!

PLUS, your hunting buddies and Poco Gun Club members and Helga D. miss you too…

Contents

GREAT HUNTING ADVENTURES	iii
DEDICATION	v
Acknowledgements	a
Preface	b
Introduction	e
1952	1
Chapter 1:	2
My First Hunt —and Almost My Last	2
1955	23
Chapter 2:	24
Coquihalla Goat Hunt	24
1958	49
Chapter 3:	49
Partners for Better or Worse	49
1959	71
Chapter 4:	71
Grouse: The Best Booby Prize	71

1964	83
Chapter 5:	83
A Bear for Papa	83
1967	100
Chapter 6:	100
Tatlayoko Lake Deer Hunt	100
1969	116
Chapter 7:	116
The Poachers	116
1970	132
Chapter 8:	132
Ashnola Sheep Hunt	132
1971	144
Chapter 9:	144
West Kootenay Safari: The Author's Jackpot	144
1974	158
Chapter 10:	159
Moose Hunt at Fish Lake	159
1980	178

Chapter 11:	**178**
Maybe Tomorrow	**178**
About the Author	**192**
Endnotes	**195**
A Few Photos:	**197**
CONTACT ME:	**213**

Acknowledgements

I would like to acknowledge the accepted wisdom of all sportsmen and women who recognize that hunting is not an idle past time nor, God forbid, just a sport. Rather it is a love for the creatures of the wild and the fair chase that are important to any thinking hunter. In particular I would like to acknowledge all my partners who through the years I've had the pleasure to associate with and whose good company has helped to make the writing of these stories a labour of love. They are too numerous to name individually, but none are forgotten.

My special thanks go to Jim Railton and the late Ed Meade; both encouraged me in my early attempts to write about my hunting experiences. I also thank Will Dawson who patiently helped me understand the basics of writing in a "foreign language". Thanks also to Lorraine Harris, a colleague who has always been a most helpful, constructive critic along with my daughter Hella, who helped me with my writing from the time she was about 8 years old because I was learning to write my stories as a second language just as she was learning to write as well.

Preface

A top-rate storyteller is rare and precious, at the pinnacle of literature. The good yarner is surpassed for some by the comedian and the clown, but the vivid story lingers longer. Such a teller of tales is Henry Prante. Prante lives in Port Coquitlam, a small city enfolded in the suburbs of the metropolis of Vancouver, British Columbia. "Poco," as the residents lovingly call their city, is a great jumping-off spot for game shooting in the wildlife-filled interior and northland of massive British Columbia.

"B.C." has lured thousands of would-be and frustrated hunters from all over the world, especially from the Germanic countries, where the standards for courteous, conservative hunting have been set and cherished for centuries. And B.C. lured Heinrich, now aka Henry, Prante in the early 1950's as a 23-year-old: he was drawn by the instinct that so many of us have been unable to resist, inherent in all men, handed down through millions of years of physical and social evolution.

I can't name the exact year, but vividly recall meeting this powerfully built, intense, quiet outdoorsman during the early fifties at a fish and game convention of the "lower mainland" region of B.C. Prante (pronounced "Pranty") was a delegate for his own Port Coquitlam and District Fish and Game Club. Despite his temporary lack of command of English, he was outspoken on hunting ethics, a subject not too well appreciated in North America in those days.

As a career outdoors writer, one of my moonlighting jobs was freelance or ghost-editing for various outdoors journals. I was astounded a few years after seeing Prante at those early wildlife meetings, to be handed the chore of editing one of his articles on shooting. It needed some polishing, all right; most articles do. But, aside from the struggle he was so rapidly winning with English, the man had that golden touch of the teller of tales, something I believe we inherit, rather than develop, which smacks of the great musical and other artistic talents. Whether or not Mr. Prante is another Shakespeare or even only a Jack O'Connor, his pen fills my nostrils with the aroma of wood smoke, the sound of a clean river gripping a canoe paddle, the sight of sunrises and sparkling water, and the chill or warmth of blizzard or campfire.

Aside from the simple but vivid prose, there

are no personal "secrets" in the author's neatly packaged shooting log. The stories appear chronologically, the earlier admitting to the faults we all showed when we started out, even an innocent brush with the law. His later hunts brought great rewards and some pointed conclusions about poachers or game hogs that Prante and partners encountered.

For those who enjoy the many aids to hunting, the author, without becoming technical, reports on trips in most kinds of watercraft and vehicle used for hunting. With him we live in motels, cabins and tents. Sometimes we share nights under the stars or in the high mountains with no shelter at all. Henry Prante in 1985 still is young. I'm confident he has many more stories in him. In fact, he just produced a similar book of B.C. tales in German and has been told it rapidly sold out over there. Let's hope we'll read more of them.

~Lee Straight

www.steelheadermag.com/lelandstraight.html

Introduction

Ever since I was old enough to read books and hunting literature it has been my dream to roam the trackless wilderness of Canada; to hunt wild game, to climb tall mountains and to paddle my own graceful canoe over clear waters teeming with fish and fowl.

In 1952 that dream became reality when I moved to British Columbia from Germany with my family and established myself as a builder of boats and yachts. It was not easy to raise four children and to follow my dreams of exploring the British Columbia wilderness, photographing it, hunting and writing about it, at every given opportunity. Financially it was more difficult than I had imagined, but worked extra to scrape up the funds needed and I have no regrets.

For over 30 years now I have hunted in B.C. on countless trips through some of the finest hunting country the western world has to offer. I travelled by car, 4x4 truck, trail bike, horse, canoe or river boat, by aircraft and even freight train to reach my hunting ranges. I have climbed from sea level to the summits of sky-scraping mountains and have hunted every species of game this province has to offer.

It was tough going at times, hair-raising, even dangerous but it was all highly dramatic and beautiful. To find game was, of course, always the excuse to get away into the wilderness. To kill game was, of lesser importance unless I needed venison for the family.

Perhaps I should confess that my hunting philosophy is really that of a livestock farmer who cares for his animals and culls his herd only to make a living — or to protect the range and propagate only the best of his stock. **Thus I have never been a trophy hunter.**

But I have, on occasion, killed trophy-sized game. My greatest reward of the hunt was always the unforgettable adventure of living on raw land, in harmony with nature or against all odds.

Who would not enjoy the view from the top of the Yalakom Mountains, or the Ashnola region's glistening lakes where one can bump into a California bighorn ram, a mountain goat or mule deer among brilliant autumn colors reflected in mirror-shiny waters? Who would not enjoy living, if only for a brief span, in the swamp and water world of the Atlin region where the largest of our moose roam, where mountain caribou and stone sheep often stand etched against an azure sky in unbelievably sharp detail? And who would not enjoy a trip along the turning and twisting Coquihalla River as it winds its tortuous course through deep canyons gleaming like molten silver in the light of a harvest moon? Who would not love to ride a sure-footed saddle horse and feel at one with nature?

These are unforgettable experiences for me, bound together by the companionship of good partners. Indeed, when others stop along our crowded highways to stare at nature, it is the hunter who truly lives the experience as he sits near a game trail and waits for his quarry. He sees the life and death experience in true perspective. He might observe a grizzly grazing in a meadow or digging for marmots or hear the bugle of a rutting bull elk; the dry cough of a bull moose. He goes to sleep with the chorus of timber wolves singing him a lullaby, yet he also knows that the song probably means death for some creature unlucky enough to cross the wolves.

I suppose I am a sentimentalist because these are the things I crave most. Of course, I have killed plenty of game but I never was wasteful and our family and friends ate the meat. I could never bear to see someone discard a killed animal. Whenever a moose or other big game animal was too far to transport for salvage, it was left to go its way.

I have always worked hard and spared no expense to recover my game to ensure that it had not died in vain. My trophy wall does not show the bragging-size horns and antlers of prime breeding stock, simply because I always wish to return to find the woods and wildlife healthy and plentiful.

Times have changed since my early hunting days. Good hunting partners have died or faded away; new partners have come along and they too have greatly contributed to my enjoyment of the great outdoors. Sometimes, though, things did not work out as well as they might have. Still, to give an accurate account of what hunting in British Columbia is all about I have included such experiences. To avoid embarrassment I have changed the names of some of those involved because it has never been my style to ridicule or belittle a friend no matter how deserving said friend might have been. If my revelations do cause someone discomfort, I apologize because it is not intended.**~Henry**

1952

In the late fall of 1952 I had my first hunting adventure in British Columbia. As a descendant of an old, German ship-building family, on my mother's side, and farming-hunting stock on my father's, I was happy to be in Vancouver where I was close to both sea and forest. It is hardly surprising, too, that I should have thought of combining boating with hunting.

It was only a matter of time before I learned that deer roamed the coastal islands. I built myself a small boat and saved enough for a Mod. 98 k army surplus rifle. When hunting season came, a friend loaned me a single barrel break action shotgun. Of course, I had already purchased a $12 Alien-Resident hunting licence and two deer tags for 50¢ each. I was ready... or so I thought.

Chapter 1:

My First Hunt — and Almost My Last

The clear waters of Howe Sound were mirror smooth and the November sun had just sunk behind the snow dusted mountains of the Sechelt Peninsula. For the third time my little outboard motor began to stutter for no apparent reason. Luckily, when it quit I was within a few hundred yards of the rocky shores of an island.

"Only a quarter-mile to go," I thought, "That's not bad. I'll row to shore and there, somehow, I'll fix that troublesome engine because if I can't I'll have to row all the way back to Garrow Bay."

Alone in the boat, I silently took stock of my situation. I checked the supplies that would have to last me until I returned home: a little butter and a few slices of bread and cheese - leftovers from my lunch. When I'd set out I hadn't thought I would need anything else.

But that had been in the morning, at first light. That morning I had many happy thoughts. It was wonderful to putter on the smooth ocean and inhale the pungent salt air, to feel the breeze on my face. I don't suppose any captain on the 7 seas were ever happier than I was at that moment. The high mountains of the Coast Range glistened with the first white of winter. Not a cloud marred the beauty of the deep blue sky. But then the waters of the Pacific Ocean began to play tricks on me. A wind came up from nowhere and a half hour later the sea was suddenly so rough that I made little headway. Large waves rolled towards me, their foamy tops hissing as they passed under the keel. I contemplated turning back then, but didn't dare for fear of capsizing.

About 10 a.m. the motor had stalled for the first time and I was forced to row for an hour to keep from being swamped.

Throughout the day the wind continued to play tricks on me. When it finally subsided I had drifted, rowed or motored so close to an island that I could no longer consider turning about.

I had no maps or charts of the area, not even a compass. "Why would I need that stuff?" I'd thought before leaving home. "All those islands are plainly visible. You can't get lost on little old Howe Sound."

When the motor had quit for the second time the sun was starting to set. After many pulls that frayed the starter rope it fired up one more time. I looked up from my labours then and noticed some white cliffs on my starboard beam where a half dozen chubby seals and a colony of cormorants eyed me curiously - surely wondering why I had cursed so loudly. Watching them, I had made some progress towards shore before the sun set and the engine finally quit for good.

I started rowing towards land then, thinking that I would have to spend the night somewhere and wondering how that was to be done. "There must be a hollow tree here," I thought, "If there's not, I'll have to build a little shelter of some kind, make a big fire and enjoy it all." Aside from shelter, my main concern was for my wife and two-year-old daughter at home who would wait up for me and worry.

Suddenly I heard a human voice. I turned around to see where it came from and saw the outline of a cabin among the trees on shore. Blue smoke drifted from a chimney and on the beach of the little bay stood a man who continued to call out to me. I was surprised. I had not expected the island to be inhabited. I aimed the boat for the man on the beach. As I got closer I could see that he was elderly. "What are you looking for?" he called.

My command of the English language was not nearly as good as it should have been and I had to formulate an answer rather slowly. Meanwhile, I reached the beach, where the old man grabbed the painter and dragged the boat onto solid ground. Then he saw the guns lying in the boat. "Are you a hunter?" he asked.

I nodded.

He tied the boat to a large chunk of beached driftwood, muttered something about "tides" and said that they would not come high enough overnight to take my boat away.

"When I saw you coming I put on the kettle. Coffee ought to be ready now. Bring your gear and come on in." Then he just turned and walked towards the cabin. I followed. The house was brown. Its paint was peeling in a few spots and a little black and white dog sat on the door sill, growling. "That's Patsy," said my host, "she helps me pass the time around here."

The cabin was simply furnished, but very clean and cozy. In the old-fashioned woodstove crackled a warming fire and before I knew it a steaming cup of coffee was thrust into my hands. Only when I drank it did I realize how cold I had been. I still shivered.

The old man introduced himself. Alvin was his name and he said that I was lucky to have found him here.

"Usually I live on the other side of the bay. This is just a summer camp and I'm caretaker for absent owners. I used to be a miner, at Britannia, but now I'm retired and live on the island all year around." He wrinkled his brow and shook his. "I've never seen anyone in such a small boat come over here from the mainland. Certainly not this time of year anyhow. This sound is not a duck pond, you know. When the Squamish wind blows not even the water taxi from Horseshoe Bay will come out to bring my groceries."

The old man continued to talk, never waiting for an answer to his questions. After the introductions I hardly said anything. Apparently, he had not had a chance to speak to anyone for some time. And while he was always polite, he was not entirely complimentary. He constantly berated me in the third person. He lamented someone's" ignorance "for crossing deep and potentially dangerous waters in a little "bucket", for being dumb. But despite the old man's peculiarities, I did have the feeling that I was most welcome.

"Where had you planned to sleep, huh? Maybe outside in the cold? Under a tree maybe? Only a dummy will sleep under a tree. I have two soft, warm beds in here - you stay, eh?"

"I'll manage," I said. "No, you won't!" came his surprisingly strong contradiction.

I was puzzled by this man, but considering my alternatives I agreed with him and thanked him for his invitation. Meanwhile it grew dark outside. Through the kitchen window I enjoyed a great view of the sea, the twinkling lights of Horseshoe Bay and the moving navigational lights of boats and ships. A brilliantly lit ferry steamed across the sound on a westward course. I thought it was the Black Ball ferry on its way to Gibson's or Nanaimo.

The old man began to fumble with a gas lantern, something I had never seen before. He pumped pressure into the tank, held a burning match near the white globe and with a sudden "plop" filled the whole room with yellow, hissing light. "Suppertime," he said.

He put more wood on the fire and set a few pots on the stove. "There isn't a hell of a lot to eat around here," he said with a grin. "The water taxi should have come day before yesterday. But for now it's enough. If you shoot a deer in the morning we'll have plenty of fresh meat anyway, eh?"

He paused for a moment and then looked at me with the sorry, dead-serious face of an undertaker. "You do know how to shoot a deer?"

"Of course," I lied. "Heard there were lots of deer on Gambier Island."

"Gambier?" the old man scratched his head.

"You don't have to go there. We have enough of them right here."

I must have looked puzzled because he spoke again. "You think you're on Gambier Island?" "Yeah, where else could I be?"

"On Anvil Island, my boy. You sure did get turned around, didn't you?" Alvin grinned now as if he had heard a good joke. "We don't have as many deer as Gambier, but there are enough for you to practise on. Sure hope you don't foul up, though, otherwise we might get kinda hungry."

I felt like a complete fool then. Where and when did I get off course? I recalled having crossed what I took to be a huge bay where the wind pushed me around considerably. As I sat watching the old man cook our dinner and smelled the good food, I was as embarrassed as a teenager without a driving license; but I was still glad to be on the island, even if it was the wrong one.

"God knows if there is such a warm, friendly place with a resident cook on that damn Gambier Island," I thought, trying as best I could to hide my embarrassment.

While the old man cooked Irish stew he asked what kind of trouble I had with the motor. I didn't know that either, in fact I had no earthly idea how I was going to make it run again.

"I'm not a mechanic," I said. "The friend who lent me the motor assured me it would run perfectly, that it was in first class condition."

"Sure, people always say that," my new friend ventured, "but have you got tools to fix it?"

"No," I answered truthfully, but withheld my original thought - "I don't know anything about outboards. With tools I might make things worse rather than better." "I'll lend you some tools in the morning," he offered. This stew was very tasty. The old man had served boiled potatoes with it, some vegetables and a bottle of beer for each of us. He said it was the last beer he had in the house.

I didn't really know how to express my gratitude towards him. He was the most generous person I had met since coming to Canada. After dinner I continued to worry about my wife. She had not been happy to see me go alone into what she only too rightly perceived to be raw wilderness.

"She must think I've drowned, or that I've a broken leg, or that some wild animal has eaten me. In the morning she'll call the police for sure. Someone is going to come looking for my remains sometime."

My thoughts were suddenly interrupted by Patsy's low growl. The old man, said, "Yup, there'll be some deer on the point in the morning. When Patsy acts like this, it means deer are sneaking past the house. They love to go where the bush is not too thick.

The "point" is the best feeding area for them on the whole island. But don't you miss, you hear! I see the barometer is falling like crazy. There's another storm on its way. You'll have to stay a while longer. So, if you want to eat well, bring me a deer."

The barometer was accurate in its prediction. When the old man woke me in the morning it was still dark. A strong wind buffeted the house and rattled the window panes; sometimes it blew smoke back out of the stove.

While we ate breakfast I looked out at the sound. Our bay looked calm enough, but farther out the sea was capped in the now familiar white. As daylight grew stronger it seemed the water was boiling.

As far as I could see there was only black water and snowy foam.

The old man grinned. "What did I tell you, eh? It's no day for boating. Just go out, get your deer and then we'll see what happens."

I had no choice in the matter. In any event, I did want to hunt and experience the romance of it all. I wanted to try my rifle on real game and not just paper targets.

"How will it perform?" I pondered, "How will I? I don't want to become even more of a laughing stock than I am now."

The coast or Columbian black-tailed deer, Odocoileus hemionus columbianus, is a close cousin to the larger mule deer of the B.C. mainland. This much I had read about the species I was about to hunt. I knew that deer are good swimmers and thus populate most islands of the Pacific coast of North America.

I knew that they have few natural enemies on the smaller islands, but that they do sometimes outstrip their food supply. I also knew that deer love to browse on all kinds of berry shrubs, vine maple, hazelnut and mountain ash, as well as on dogwood, cedar, hemlock and fir; and that one of their favourite foods is mistletoe.

As I walked out of the cabin, I sincerely hoped my knowledge would help me bag a good buck.

I loaded my rifle and set out to hunt. The island was quite rocky and in places densely covered with underbrush. New to Canada, I did not recognize most floras. I knew that B.C. trees supplied excellent lumber, although in the raw wild I couldn't tell one species from another. Most of them simply looked like overgrown Christmas trees to me.

But I didn't have to walk through much of the unidentified forest. Just 100 yards from the cabin I saw my first deer. It was a buck, too. He stood on a pile of rocks looking toward two fat does that browsed on some bushes.

Remembering the old man's advice I simply aimed the rifle and fired. The buck dropped as if hit by a sledge hammer, the does fled in leaps and bounds for heavy cover.

I got excited. My God was I nervous. I stumbled and fell a few times, skinning my shins as I made my way to the fallen buck. There I stood in awe of what I'd done. Such a beautiful creature. In my excitement I hadn't noticed that the old man had followed me. He suddenly laid a hand on my shoulder to congratulate me—and I nearly jumped out of my boots.

"Not a bad shot," he said as he examined the animal. "Not bad at all. You didn't spoil an ounce of meat. Well, at least you can shoot, huh? For lunch we'll have fried liver 'n boiled spuds."

The whole carcass weighed no more than 100 pounds. The buck's antlers were smallish and had only three short tines on each beam.

"No great trophy, this," I thought.

The old man must have read my mind. "Don't worry about them horns," he said, "we can't eat them anyway."

The old man did not waste time. He had his knife out and dressed the carcass quickly. Together we dragged the buck to the woodshed and hung him to cool. I was duly impressed with such quick work and glad that he had done it — in fact, he had shown me what I didn't know without making me expose my ignorance further. I really liked and appreciated that guy.

After we enjoyed the liver at lunch, I tried to get the old man to help me with the motor repair. He shook his head.

"Nope, don't know anything about those things either. But I'll get you the tools. You have plenty of time now, "you'd never make it home today anyway."

Four full days I fooled around on that damn motor until suddenly sputtered back to life. I didn't know why the engine ran again, unless the little plug of matted material I had pulled from the gas line had been my problem all along. The old man seemed to think so. Anyway, it now purred like a kitten. It was only an 11/2 h.p. motor and at the best of times it would give the boat a top speed of perhaps 2 1/2 knots.

During the four days I'd worked on the engine, the old man just watched me from his kitchen window. At meal times, he served good food and was friendly. He had heard the engine fire up and run and when I came inside to clean up he had a stack of papers lying on the table. There were charts and a booklet filled with graphs and tables. I didn't understand any of it. He pointed at the book. "Eh, kid, you can't leave here before tomorrow morning; — 10 a.m. at the earliest. You'll have to go with the tide, or the current will take you all the way up the sound to Britannia Beach or Squamish."

I didn't really have a clue where these places were in relation to where we were, but he showed me on the charts and explained how tides would influence my journey. I became worried but I was determined to get home.

The next morning I was packed up early. I left half the buck for the old man and promised to speak to the captain of the water taxi to bring him his supplies in a hurry. The old man shook his head.

"It's better you wait for the taxi yourself," he said. "When he comes — any time now — will take you and your boat home."

Considering I am a hard-headed Kraut, I no longer wanted to listen to the old man. I just felt I had to go home. During the past days I had seen some big boats cruising the sound; I was certain they were searching for me. At that moment, as if to strengthen my determination, a small float plane droned over the island on course for Gambier. Way out on the water I could see the odd whitecap glisten. From a distance the water did not look very dangerous.

"The barometer is still falling," warned the old man. "The real storm is still coming! If you leave now you will likely never get home again."

The old man was sincerely concerned for me. He didn't help me to launch the boat on what he thought was a dangerous mission. As I thanked him one last time for his generosity and started the engine, he stood quietly in front of the cabin and shook his balding head. Patsy barked as if she too wanted me to stay. Yes, they were my good friends indeed.

I had charted my homeward course quietly and only in my mind. I wanted to travel as far as I could in the lee of the island and then follow the shoreline of Gambier Island toward Bowen Island and the ferry route. From there I only had to cross over to Garrow Bay. If the weather got really bad, I trusted that one of the ferries might help out. Not wanting to be laughed at, I had told the old man nothing of this scheme.

The first mile was easy. The seas were calm. Then, as I neared Gambier's shore, the boat began a wild dance. I looked back and momentarily forgot to breathe. Uncountable rows of whitecaps threatened to overtake and overturn me. I searched the shore for a safe haven. All was rocky and rough and the surf battered itself into atoms of white spray.

The little engine purred away. Even at full throttle it did not get excited or give more speed. Each following wave gave me a push that threatened to capsize the boat.

"The damn thing's gonna flip!" I thought.

In desperation I was forced to steer a violently erratic course. Some waves were six feet tall. Foam blew about my head. Spray slopped into the boat. Because I had covered all my gear with my raincoat I got drenched. As each wave passed under the keel it would hold the boat for a moment before slamming it into the trough. The old man's words were constantly running through my mind: "You'll never make it, my boy."

I thought of my wife, my small daughter, Hella. "What will happen to them in this wild land without me and any other relatives from Germany here?" I started to pray and I steered like a robot. Straight ahead…. hard to port…. straight ahead again.

A great wave suddenly sloshed over the stern and I found myself sitting in water. Water sloshed about my feet as the boat's floorboards floated about. Splasssshh. Another big wave came aboard. The motor sputtered badly, its' spark plug wet. After a couple of long seconds it calmed down and went back to a steady purr.

Despairing, I jumped amid ships and grabbed for the oars. The boat rode the sea much better now and when I found that the motor stayed on a straight course, I bailed the boat with one hand while manipulating an oar with the other. Somehow I got rid of most of the bilge water.

I didn't know how many hours had passed since I left Anvil Island. I realized that I was now in the ferry lanes - but where were the ferries? Then the motor stopped. The fuel tank was empty and needed refilling. I had enough gasoline with me, more than enough to get me home; the problem was getting it into the tank. I balanced precariously on the stern seat and poured more gas into the ocean than into the tank. Because the water splashed wildly about, I couldn't prevent a few sips of salt water from getting into the tank.

I drifted broadside to the big waves and was unable to prevent it. I recall being surprised that I did not capsize immediately. The boat rolled like a drunken sailor in the gutter of skid road, but hardly any water came over the sides. For an hour I tried to restart the engine.

No luck. It wouldn't fire up. Then a wave splashed over the port gunwale and I bailed like a madman.

All my gear floated about in the bilge and got in the way of the bailing can. I was wet to the skin and feeling like hypothermia had set in. As I looked up momentarily to bring the boat back on course I saw it: salvation. Or so I prayed.

A large blue-grey boat came out of the narrows from the west as if it had followed me. It flew the Canadian flag. It was a police boat. But as I watched, even this big ship had its' own troubles; it fought the seas like a free-style swimmer. In the cabin I saw the silhouette of the pilot at the helm.

"In a moment he'll see me. He must see me. Please mister looks this way!"

I stood up in spite of the rolling motion and waved at him. I yelled too. As suddenly as it had come the police boat turned and headed for Horseshoe Bay. They hadn't seen me!

In a wild panic I grabbed the shotgun, poured the water out of its barrel, loaded it and fired a signal shot into the air. The boat continued on its course. They hadn't heard the shot.

I loaded a second shell - buckshot - aimed straight at the boat and fired. I thought I could hear the lead strike the cabin, but the boat steamed on. I was devastated and felt totally abandoned to the mercy of the sea."This is what it feels like to prepare to die," I thought. Then, out of utter frustration, I gave the starter rope one more violent pull.

Ra-ta-ta-ta-tat. The damn thing started again as if nothing had had been wrong. I was alone on the wild sea, but I had the power to go somewhere. Letting the motor run on its' own, I worked with both oars to help it out. Leaning into the oars my fighting spirit returned.

I watched the seas like a hawk now and aimed to miss the largest waves by trying to brake the oar to let one pass ahead of me or by rowing like hell to get out from under one. At times I thought my back would break, and the boat still rolled as if it wished to tip over.

Stop. Go. Stop. Go. I don't recall how long I rowed like a robot. The waves became suddenly smaller and finally in the lee of a point of land the sea calmed completely. It took some time to comprehend this miracle. When I turned about to look I saw the entrance of Garrow Bay before me. I steered for the nearest float and tied up to it. Then I stumbled on numb feet to shore. On a driftwood stump I sat down and with stiff fingers rolled a cigarette.

"Finally. Safe. I'll get home after all!" This is all I thought while I sat and smoked.

When I carried my gear ashore the marina operator came to meet me. He asked me who I was.

"Jesus Christ, man!" he almost choked, when I told him who I was. "We've searched the whole week for you. Where the hell were you?"

He shook his head when I said Anvil Island. "What, in this weather?"

Through chattering teeth I told him what had happened. He led me into his home to warm up and call the authorities.

Of course, I never told him or anyone else that I had shot at that police boat. That part of the story was my secret, until now.

Finally came the hardest part of the whole hunting trip. I called my wife.

1955

This story requires some explanation because, in addition to describing mountain goat hunting, this story was also my first endeavour in outdoor writing. After the hunt described on the following pages, I made a careless remark to my partner about a hunting story I'd read, and boasted, "I can probably do better than that myself."

I should have known better. Despite the fact that I was still on "fighting" terms with the English language, my partner urged me to write about the goats of the Coquihalla. Later, when I met Jim Railton of The Northwest Sportsman and mentioned that I didn't think there was enough educational material being published for greenhorn hunters, he suggested I give the writing business a try. Well I did, and here it is.

Chapter 2:
Coquihalla Goat Hunt

It was during my hunting "apprenticeship" that the late Rudy Schultheiss and I decided to try mountain goat hunting. With our eagerness to learn, coupled with our unbridled enthusiasm, we often took some hard knocks. On more than one occasion our Canadian-born friends laughed until they cried over our ignorance and innocence.

One friend used to say quite openly, "You and Rudy have rocks in your heads."

Maybe so, but how could we learn anything without trying? There was no such thing as a hunter training course or manual. We read everything we could about hunting and, therefore, unfortunately, learned a lot of nonsense.

Even as late as 1955 it wasn't always easy to distinguish between fact and fiction; thus we had decided to rely on information from friends and acquaintances rather than books. But even these sources often led us astray.

One September evening in 1955 Rudy knocked at my door to say that he had finally found a good place to hunt goats.

He was excited, as he usually was when planning a hunt.

"Where did you hear about this place?" I asked.

"I heard about it from Albert. Albert said there are plenty of goats. And I know how we can get there."

"Albert? Albert who?"

"The prospector. You know him. He's Bill Richardson's friend and used to prospect in his younger years. Albert knows every mountain in B.C., before prospecting he worked in bridge construction, for the railway. Yesterday he told me everything we need to know." Rudy grinned as if he had won the Irish Sweepstake. "Hey! Are you listening?"

I most certainly was listening. I knew Albert — a nice fellow, a real gentleman. And Bill Richardson had made my brand-new 30-06 Mauser for me. He was a reputable sort and quite well known in hunter circles.

"There's no road into the mountains Albert told me about, but there is a little-known rail line," said Rudy. "It's called the Kettle Valley Line. Belongs to the C.P.R. We can go hunting by train. What do you think? Wanna go this coming weekend?"

"And Albert told you exactly how to get there?"

"Sure did. He said we could shoot the goats right off the railway tracks, no problem."

Rudy's story sounded too good to be true but I couldn't turn down this trip. So I started planning too. Both of us had seen goats before, but only from a distance. Each time we began a hunt, the goats were on top of some awfully tall mountains, and you could only reach them with field glasses. I had some theoretical knowledge about goats. I knew they weren't related to the domestic goat, but rather to the antelope.

According to Game Department figures, B.C. contained about 100,000 of them, scattered about the mountain ranges of the province. From the U.S. border to the Yukon, goats can be found. But whether a hunter was lucky enough to bag one would depend on a few trifling facts, such as his own physical condition, determination, ability to shoot well, and lastly, his ration of luck.

I had also read some goat literature by the late Grancel Fitz of Boone and Crocket Club fame, in which he expressed the view that Rocky Mountain goats are probably the most dangerous game. He wrote that a big 'billy' could, under the right conditions, fight a grizzly and win. I have since met folks who claim to have witnessed such a duel and maintain that they saw a 'billy' push a bear right off a cliff.

While I am still skeptical about this particular story, my subsequent experience confirmed that Grancel Fitz knew a lot about goats and the dangerous mountain environment they inhabit. The hunter has only to slip once, just as a good friend of mine did — George Hoy of Richmond, B.C. — to meet a tragic end.

The day Rudy and I outfitted ourselves to hunt the goats of the Coquihalla Pass we had no real idea of the dangers that lay ahead of us. But while we were complete greenhorns, I would take any bet that the Canadian Pacific Railway and the majestic mountains along the Coquihalla River never saw more dedicated hunters. Needless to say, we didn't stay 'green' for long — at the end of our adventure we were black and blue from the bumps and bruises of experience.

The following weekend we packed our gear into my old Ford sedan and drove to the C.P.R. station in downtown Vancouver to take the train to Iago. Iago was the magic place we were told. A section crew was stationed there and the crew members would show us where the goats were. Maybe we just daydreamed too long on our drive to the train station or outright miscalculated our travel time, but we got stuck in heavy weekend traffic and missed the train.

"That's alright," said the ever optimistic Rudy. "We can just drive the car to Hope and catch the train there. It's only 100 miles to Hope- we can catch that train if you step on it." Knowing that there was only one passenger train a day making the Kettle Valley trip, I agreed to Rudy's plan.

We drove off in pursuit of that train. Luckily, we weren't caught for speeding. But when we arrived in Hope we saw only the tail lights of the train. It was gone.

We were standing outside the station building discussing what to do with our weekend, when a railway worker who had overheard our conversation recommended that we drive to the next station.

"It's called Othello. The train has to travel up a fairly steep grade with lots of curves, but the road up there isn't too bad. And it's only six miles. I'm sure you can make it." Into the car and away we went. It was obviously not the intelligent thing to do - racing a train along a strange gravel road in the dark- and we knew it. But we were, as I've said, dedicated and determined and perhaps a bit nuts to boot.

Just as we reached the station the three heavy diesels crawled into view. Rudy grabbed the stop flag from the station building, stood on the tracks and waved according to the instructions posted on the station wall. The train stopped. "All we need to do now is to outsmart those goats," I crowed. Two minutes later the train pulled out again - and left us standing there. No one had opened a door for us.

A superstitious person would have quit that goat hunt right then. We, however, were not superstitious. We just wanted to go hunting and nothing else would do. But first, Rudy planned to return to Hope and make a formal complaint to the C.P.R.

"Schweinerei!" he yelled in his Swiss-German dialect.

"Too lazy to open the doors for fare-paying passengers. That conductor must've been sleeping already. I'll let them know how I feel about the way they run their railroad!"

When we arrived back in Hope the station building was empty but the waiting room was open. "Okay," Rudy said, "guess we'll just camp right here until the station master comes back. Give me a hand with our gear so we can cook a good supper. I'm starving.

At about 6 a.m. when the station master showed up again, ready to throw us out. "What do you think this is… a gypsy camp? Out you go!"

A noisy and heated debate followed. There was, first of all, Rudy's "Schwyzer-Deutsch," followed by the Italian dialect of the railway man, and finally my own mix of low German and English. When the dust finally settled, the poor railroader sat between us on a bench, drank a cup of our coffee and promised to put us aboard the next freight bound for Penticton.

"You will be aboard in two hours, fellows. It's a long train and will take all day to get you to the Coquihalla Pass, but if you want go hunting that badly - sure, you can have a ride. I just wish I could come along with you."

It was a wonderful arrangement all around. Who wouldn't jump at the chance to ride a big locomotive?

Once aboard we discovered that all of the 35 miles to Iago were uphill. We could almost have walked as fast as the train moved along the winding tracks above the Coquihalla River.

There were tunnels galore and snow sheds and bridges that seemed as fragile as spider webs crossing deep gorges and valleys. Our train was like a caterpillar crawling up straight rock faces. I felt nauseated looking into the abyss of the deep canyon. On this stretch, the engineer said, the train had to climb from sea level to about 3,000 feet — the steepest rail grade anywhere on the North American continent.

Towards evening, the train reached Iago. The engineer said it would be too much trouble to stop the train and get it started again so we just grabbed our few things and jumped off.

Iago consisted of one house containing a C.P.R. office, a few small sheds, a work train that stood on a siding, and a small private home that belonged to an elderly Chinese watchman, Mr. Wong.

It was a friendly place. The section crew even extended an invitation to camp in their train or in an empty boxcar, but we were happy to pitch our tent. After we rolled out the bedrolls and cooked dinner, Mr. Wong arrived to say hello.

He was extremely polite and seemed to enjoy a certain special status among the crew. Most of them were of Italian or Portuguese ancestry, with names like Antonio, Guiseppe,

Alfredo, Fernando and Mario — names they casually bandied about in a chaos of dialects. But Mr. Wong was always Mister Wong.

For 30 years Mr. Wong had lived in Iago. He told us, as well as he could in his own version of English, that he had already "shot all goats dead."

"Goats gone. Grizzly all gone too." He grinned and added, "I shoot all." He showed us his rifle that had done the damage. It was a Savage.

We enjoyed trying to understand Mr. Wong. Someone told us that he had come to Canada as a young man and arrived in Iago directly from China. He had not had the opportunity to learn the English language as well as he might have, but he was a proud and successful hunter, eager to chat about his exploits.

Under any other circumstances we would have enjoyed this visit tremendously. But after we had come such a long way with so much difficulty, Mr. Wong's disclosures about ridding the area of game did not raise our spirits. We looked at each other and shrugged.

"What now?" I asked.

Everyone we talked to in the section crew had a different opinion. Finally, the section boss came and said that he knew a spot where two American hunters had killed goats some time earlier.

"How far from here?" we asked.

"Four miles," said another fellow. He was a watchman and had to patrol the tracks ahead of the trains and ensure no trees, rocks or other avalanche material would cause accidents. His work took him over the four miles to Romeo.

"One of you can come with me tonight," he offered. "It's almost a full moon, so I can show you the area. We'll take the speeder."

Rudy was tired, but urged me to go check it out anyway. So, at 11 p.m. we set off. It was a long four miles. I soon discovered that my new "friend" hadn't asked me along out of kindness alone: he only had a hand-operated speeder and wanted someone to help him push the peculiar contraption uphill. So while my friend rode in the back seat, I pumped the driver-bar back and forth to move the speeder - which was far from fast.

In our hour's ride we crossed many bridges that didn't even have planks between the tracks - an eerie experience that made me fear a rapid descent through the crystal clear atmosphere. We entered many tunnels where water dripped constantly from the black ceilings.

The night was clear and warm. A pale moon climbed above the ridge on our right and the Coquihalla River glinted like solid silver in the moonlight. It was flowing far below us but we could still hear the rush of turbulent waters. From behind, my friend "entertained" me with stories of huge avalanches that would sometimes, without warning, thunder onto the racks and derail trains - and speeders, I assumed.

Near Romeo we reached the end of my guide's territory. We dismounted, lifted the speeder off the tracks and waited for the passenger train from Vancouver. By then it was midnight.

For light we had one old, smelly coal oil lantern that illuminated our immediate surroundings. After the passenger train rumbled past we moved the speeder back on the track, facing homeward.

Clickety-clack, clickety-clack. Without effort we began to roll, faster and faster. My friend let go of the driver-bar and the wooden beast that I had pushed up the mountain came alive. No train could have travelled at our speed - it would have jumped the rails for certain.

I guessed that we were travelling faster than 30 miles per hour. The first tunnel came at us like the dark throat of a medieval dragon ready to swallow us forthwith. Instantly we were wet, as if someone had aimed a water hose at us. On the first curve I leaned toward the mountain side of the track, but our wheels squealed too much and my new friend called, "Lean the other way, eh. She goes faster."

I clung tighter to my seat and prayed that we wouldn't jump the rails. Calick, calick, click, click, click, ratatatatat. Over the bridge! Shush and past the first waterfall.

My eyes were squeezed shut, but I felt the cold breath and the fine spray of the water. I wondered what would happen if we jumped track on one of the bridges. Would anybody find us? "Wer reitet so schnell durch Nacht und Wind?"

"Who rides so fast through night and wind?" I thought about that famous poem "Erlkloenig" by Friederich Von Schiller.

Rudy was sleeping soundly when I crawled into my sleeping bag. I shivered like a frightened puppy dog. "Thank God," I thought. "I'll never have to do that again." All night I dreamt of a circus that featured me roller skating on a tightrope. So, when the section boss awoke us it was 5:30 a.m. and I was drenched with sweat. "Hey! You guys wanna ride to Romeo?" he asked.

"A ride? What kind of ride?" I asked.

He laughed. "Don't worry, we'll take the car and we won't go fast either. We'll have to check the tracks for loose ties and rails and replace nails."

I had to assume that my night watchman friend had told his boss of the fun he'd had with me. Right after breakfast we drove off. It was uncanny but in daylight the grade looked even more sinister. A half-hour later we got off to begin our hunt.

The crew boss pointed to the other side of the canyon, to a high mountain and said

"There, that's the place." To reach the spot indicated we would have to descend into the canyon, cross the Coquihalla on a fallen log, and then climb.

While we fought our way through bushes and over boulders Rudy decided to share some of his goat "knowledge" and "expertise" with me. He'd read somewhere that a goat hunter must always approach his game from above, since goats can out climb anyone or anything. When goats detect danger they immediately move uphill. Rudy went on to explain that "when goats see a hunter above them, they'll come right to him."

In later years I learned that this was a theory only. I learned too, that a hunter should always be certain a goat is actually present before setting out to hunt. These days I refuse to climb through thorns, devil's club, alder thickets and thistles, or over still-moving rock slides for thousands of feet, if I haven't already spotted a goat from below.

The day of our first goat hunt promised to be hot. The September sun burned down from a clear sky. By noon the rocks threw back heat. When we found a trickle of water in a ravine we were attacked by hordes of flies and mosquitoes.

They defended that water with their very lives, practically driving us the rest of the way uphill. At 3 p.m. we reached the summit plateau where a constant breeze kept the devils in check.

The spot we reached was above timberline and almost bare. There was some grass, low-stemmed juniper bushes and knee-high blueberry bushes. Two glass-clear ponds glistened in the sun. They were quite shallow and surrounded by a ten-foot wide strip of soft mud. There we found our first footprints.

Rudy studied these with considerable interest. Some prints were quite fresh but disappointed us all the same - deer tracks. We were surprised by the fact that deer would roam in what we thought was mountain goat country. I wondered how they could reach such a high plateau.

While Rudy poked about in the muck I opened our pack to help myself to some food. Then I had another surprise. Rudy had re-packed our gear while I was "scouting" the terrain with the night watchman. He figured we would be back in Iago for supper and so had only packed a few sandwiches.

However, now we were at least seven miles from our well-filled grub box and I was hungry enough to chew on a live bear.

Suddenly, Rudy was running back to me and the rifle he had left laying beside the pack. He had followed the tracks halfway around the first pond. Now he grabbed his 7mm Brno and motioned for me to be quiet.

"Grizzly bear," he murmured. "Smoking-fresh tracks!" "Mr. Wong told us they were all dead," I replied as quietly.

"Maybe you saw black bear tracks."

"Not likely," he said. "Those tracks are as big as frying pans and there's a pile of droppings, still steaming." He insisted that I too view his find. Yes, indeed, Rudy was right. From then on we were quite careful. Our rifles remained loaded and ready to shoot at all times.

Meanwhile, the sun had travelled on a fair way towards setting time. Even though we did not speak about it, we were both resigned to spending the night on the mountain - we knew we had to if we wanted a chance at bagging a goat. Hard on the mountain's eastern side we found a small snowfield next to a huge juniper and a few broken remnants of scrub pine.

The juniper was at least 30 feet in diameter and its branches could serve us as mattresses, the scrub would make good firewood. After we collected some wood and made our beds ready, we left the pack behind and went hunting.

Rudy, who liked to store all kinds of odds and ends in the pack, remarked that we'd be able to cook ourselves a goat liver in foil "complete with salt and pepper." Fresh liver certainly sounded good: I was eating handfuls of wild blueberries, but still couldn't seem to fill my stomach.

I thought a great deal about the saying, "A hungry hunter is a better hunter" and can now vouch for its validity. We searched the mountain systematically, looking behind every bush and every boulder. The field glasses were constantly in use.

"Goats." He had finally spotted them. Following Rudy's direction I saw a half-dozen in a bunch — but alas, they were on the neighbouring mountain to the west, across a deep canyon, at least two-thirds of a mile away and some 600 yards below us. Watching them now through powerful binoculars I arrived at the conclusion that we had climbed the wrong mountain. Our mountain didn't offer much in the way of goat habitat. If they ever came here it was probably only while migrating.

"Well," Rudy muttered through clenched teeth, "I guess we'll eat blueberries then. It could be worse, huh?"

A hatful of berries in my lap, I continued to scan the plateau. At 300 paces there was a suspicious-looking bush that did not, as all the others did, bend and sway in the wind.

"What do you see?" asked Rudy. He ate some berries as I handed him my pair of big glasses.

"Holy Moses! There's an elk! No, no — wait a minute — there's a whole bunch of elk!"

I lay down and looked through my rifle's scope. There were six big animals; mule deer. Each and every one a buck with antlers spread wide. They were capital animals and looked larger than life.

"They're mulies," Rudy corrected himself. "I'd never have guessed they could grow so big!"

What I had mistaken for a bush was the mass of velvety antlers. The deer lay very close together and all looked in our direction. To move closer was difficult. But if we wanted fresh liver we had to shoot from this relatively long range or get up and try walking discreetly to a better shooting position.

Rudy figured we should try the latter. "They don't know humans up here. We'll get close enough - and if not, heck, we can shoot at long range if we have to."

We agreed that we would shoot only one buck and that I, since my rifle had the telescopic sight, was to do the shooting. We thought we could carry one buck down the mountain but not two.

At 100 paces I aimed, just as the largest buck came to his feet. He must have heard my stomach growl. He made a few steps away from the herd and stood broadside for an instant. Through the scope I could see his muscles flex under the still red summer coat I knew he was about to move just as my crosswire settled on his neck.

The bullet left my barrel instantly and — still watching through the scope — I saw him fall before the rifle's recoil spoiled the picture. The other deer stood up and moved about, undecided. They looked at their fallen comrade, they stretched their legs. When we were 50 paces from them they ran off.

Reaching the buck we found it impossible to lift the heavy carcass. We estimated the weight at between 350 and 400 pounds. The velvet-covered antlers had two huge forks on each beam.

"A four-pointer," said Rudy. "The two extra points over the eyes don't count." Using my 24-

inch rifle barrel I tried to measure our trophy and found the antlers had a minimum spread of 30 inches.

As I field dressed the carcass I found inch-thick solid white fat under the hide and a body cavity filled with fat as well. "Hey! What's the matter with this liver?" Rudy held up an organ completely covered in white bubbles. I had never seen such a liver and in spite of our hunger we were not inclined to eat it.

"We'll have to fry steaks then," I said. "The rest of the meat looks healthy enough - why don't you cut a pair of steaks right now, eh ?"

Back at our camp it was already getting dark as we tried to fry the two thick steaks. We spiced them with pepper and salt and wrapped them together with a little deer fat in foil. The damn things burned up leaving meat as tough as chewing gum. Then we tried a shish kabob, but that wasn't edible either. I was beginning to feel sorry for the big buck: he'd died and been put to very little use.

With the rising of an almost-full white moon a gusting easterly wind sprang up as well. There we sat, in shirt sleeves with our teeth rattling like machine-guns. The fire was too small to warm us and there wasn't enough fuel to make it bigger.

Before long we crawled under our juniper-branch mattresses to escape the wind, returning periodically to the fire for what little warmth it provided. The whole landscape before us glistened magically in the moonlight. The snow fields shone and on the opposite peak a high fall of water glittered as it rushed into deep shadow below. We had come closer to heaven, but our hungry and cold bodies didn't appreciate the beautiful scene.

Of course we couldn't sleep. After briefly drifting into semi-consciousness we would be wakened as yet another small piece of firewood burned down and left us freezing. I can't remember another night of equal duration.

At the first glimmer of dawn a rifle shot woke me. Before I could open my eyes four more shots thundered across the plateau. Then Rudy yelled, "I got him!" I roused myself to see Rudy, his rifle still pointed at a black, still form about 40 paces away among the blueberry bushes. I threw a few sticks on the fire and in the light saw that Rudy had "got" a small tree stump.

In spite of my chattering teeth I laughed. Rudy felt insulted and only told me after I apologized that he had dreamed about the big grizzly whose footprints we had seen at the pond. In his dream the bear had been sneaking up on our camp. He awoke, saw the black shadow and fired.

After this, there was no sense in trying to continue our dozing. Every bone in my body ached from the unusual work of climbing the mountain the day before, but I made a serious effort at exercising in an attempt to restore a little body warmth.

We had more steaks on ice and tried to roast them using our last firewood - with a pressure cooker we might have been able to make the steaks palatable, but not with foil and a few coals. Finally, with much cussing I made a pot out of foil so that we could at least have a hot drink from the bouillon cubes Rudy had found in the pack. I made two tiny foil cups as well and soon we were enjoying a chicken broth. For dessert we had more blueberries.

Breakfast behind us, we were ready to hunt again. Two ptarmigan ran past the campsite and stopped to peck gravel and berries. They had moved on and just stopped for a second when two shots clipped off their heads. Rudy cleaned them and wrapped the still warm bodies in foil. An hour later, well cooked, they tasted marvelous.

After eating the ptarmigan we decided to head for home, albeit in a way that might still allow us to get a goat. This meant descending the mountain and hiking along at a lower elevation.

All began well enough. Then we hit the alder it was an arduous exercise squeezing through this tangled bush. Sometimes we had to climb on all fours along heavy branches in order to cross ravines of unfathomable depths. Before long I felt like climbing back up and retracing our original route, but the alders wouldn't allow this: they grew out of the mountainside like the quills of a porcupine. We no longer thought about goat hunting, although we saw some across the canyon, 400 to 500 yards away. I might have killed one if I'd known how to get across and pick it up and bring it back!

Rudy too had had enough. After six terrible hours we reached bottom and a fast-flowing creek that had to be crossed many times.

When we reached Iago again it was late evening. The last four-mile hike had nearly killed me. I was even too tired to eat; we went to sleep immediately in our warm bedrolls — the ones we had neglected to take up the mountain.

In the morning the section boss stopped the returning passenger train for us. In the dining car we ate a meal fit for a king and swore never to hunt goats again. But we soon forgot our troubled trip. Two years later we tried again, elsewhere, and were lucky enough to bag a goat.

But this was Rudy's last goat hunt. In December of that year he drowned along with another friend, while hunting ducks on the Fraser River near Hope in December of 1957 in a canoe.

While Rudy's death was a personal tragedy for me and our family, I did have the satisfaction of knowing he had success bagging a goat once in his short lifetime.

1958

It was not an easy decision to write this story. For many years I kept it hidden away in my desk drawer. It was only when a German publishing house expressed an interest in including it in an anthology similar to this one that I decided to publish it in English as well. I trust this story is entertaining — and a little educational. I have changed the names of all concerned, so if anyone recognizes himself from my descriptions — it is not meant to be thus.

Chapter 3:

Partners for Better or Worse

I wish this story could begin with a dramatic scene featuring Jim Henders: he spots a trophy buck, squints through the rifle's telescope, he fires and the buck drops. Exciting beginning, but not one to be used for a story about Jim. "Let's go and hunt some elk," he said on the telephone one rainy October evening It was late and I was just on my way to bed when he rang. I didn't recognize his voice immediately.

"Why should I want to do a thing like that?" I replied jokingly. "And at this time of night?"

"Never mind," he answered, "get your gear ready, I'll fetch you about 5 a.m. tomorrow morning."

By now I had figured out who the caller was because no one else would make such a proposal with such deadly seriousness so late at night or so urgently.

"Damn you, Henders, couldn't you've given me a little more warning?"

"Sorry about that, old pal," he replied, "but I just know you're itching to go. And I've just learned that I've got a couple of weeks spare time coming up. Starting in the morning. Okay?"

"Alright," I grunted back. "Pick me up, but no funny stuff on this trip, you hear?" I hung up.

Next morning Jim was prompt. It still poured from the inky sky, but he smiled happily as we drove off.

"Where to, old man?" I asked.

"I'm not sure yet," he replied, "the East Kootenays, I guess."

"You're not on another wild goose chase I hope?"

"Nah. I even got a good map this time. Don't worry, I'll take you into some excellent elk country."

Knowing Jim's habits from previous hunts I wasn't too worried; but he did have me reminiscing about another elk hunt that had begun with amazingly similar plans. I couldn't help leaning back into the car's upholstery and remembering the highlights of that adventure. We had driven from our homes in Vancouver, B.C. to Williams' lake in the Cariboo, and then some considerable distance over the Bella Coola road into the Chilcotin country.

Jim had driven the whole night through and at daybreak he had selected a grassy spot to park the car. Then he had announced we were in the world's best elk country. For two days we tramped over that wonderfully open cattle range, albeit with out finding much sign of game. Then, at lunch time of the third day, Jim had come back to the car bearing a hat full of brown, dried-up, oblong pellets. He was excited as he showed them to me.

"Look," he'd said, "there must be elk nearby."

Before I could think of an appropriate answer, an old leather-face of a cowboy rode up to us. He said hello, stopped his horse to roll himself a smoke and asked what we might be hunting.

Jim, prouder than royalty, answered "Elk."

"Well now," the cowboy drawled, pokerfaced, "been livin' hereabouts all my long life — never did get to see one o' them critters yet. Never knew we had 'em in these parts." He paused a moment as if to let his message register and sighed. "Too bad, you know." Then thoughtfully he added, "But good luck to you just the same."

Looking at Jim now, driving east on Highway 401, he was obviously happy to be on a new elk-hunting adventure.

"I hope we don't meet that old cowboy again," I smirked. "And by the way— whatever became of those pellets?"

"Why don't you shut up," Jim barked. "In those days you weren't so smart either. Anyway, I had them analyzed at the university. Moose, they told me. The wife planted 'em around our rosebushes, really made 'em grow, too."

Twenty-four hours later Jim parked his car at Canal Flats' only hotel for breakfast. Chewing through a good portion of ham and eggs, he spoke between bites.

"This time, old pal, we've got it made.

Maybe I should've told you sooner, but here — take a look at this!" as he reached into his coat pocket and produced a paper the size of a dinner napkin. He pushed his plate aside and unfolded the paper before me.

A last gulp of coffee sloshed into my windpipe when I glanced at it. I choked and sputtered for a moment and Jim, impatient as always, shoved the paper right into my face. It was a most colourful thing. Wild looking blotches of brown and green indicated the Selkirk and Rocky Mountain ranges. Rivers and lakes sparkled in baby blue ink while towns and villages glowed in red. I swallowed hard but nearly choked again in a sudden fit of laughter.

This paper was no map — it was one of those propaganda sheets that a local chamber of commerce or a tourist bureau distributes. Superimposed on it were artistic renderings of animal trophy heads — goat and bear, two kinds of deer, bighorn sheep, a grizzly bear and the mighty Wapiti. The last stood with his front feet near the junction of the White and Kootenay rivers, his hind feet in Alberta, and his long belly spanning the Rockies.

Jim was dead serious. He poked a finger at the phony elk on the questionable map. "You see, this is where they are. We've caught up with 'em."

"Who told you?"

"I know a guide in these parts," he replied happily. "I wrote to him some time ago. I told him we couldn't afford his services - he's very expensive, you know- but he sent this map and some information anyway."

Jim drove another 30 miles that morning, right past the White River confluence, to an old abandoned logging camp where he quickly grabbed his rifle and left me on my own. I busied myself setting up camp in a dirty cabin. After a good cleaning job I tried out one of my self-built bunks and didn't wake again until after dark.

Shortly before 8 p.m. Jim returned.

"Let's pack up and get outta here," he grumbled, "didn't see a track of elk."

"Oh no, you don't. Don't try that stunt again. I'm staying here even if I have to hitchhike home. I've put too much effort into this camp."

"Huh." Jim sat on the bunk I'd built for him to think it over again. I gave him his portion of the fine supper I'd cooked. He stirred the food around the plate but didn't eat; he was too tired to lift the spoon.

The next morning he was in a better mood.

"We'll give it another try," he said. "We can climb these mountains and find the timberline or one of those high alpine basins the outdoor experts are always writing about. The elk are probably still up there."

Shortly after daybreak we found a crooked game trail that zig-zagged its way towards the sky. Jim climbed ahead claiming that "sooner or later we'll reach the top and then — elk watch out!"

Frozen dewdrops sparkled like squandered treasure in the morning sun. Shimmering golden tamarack were dotted among the evergreen of spruce and pine, foolhen grouse strutted in the crisp grasses. It would've been a hunter's paradise except for that trail — it was steeper than can't-afford-'em guiding fees. At noon we reached timberline and before us lay a great, snow-dusted basin.

"You see that?" asked Jim, gesturing at the grand scenery.

"These valleys really do exist!"

I had a smart remark ready for him, something like "Go find yourself another hatful," but I was exhausted and needed every breath just to stay alive. Being slightly overweight compared to Jim, I had carried an extra 60 pounds of body this far. He was in favour of climbing even higher, but I refused. Finally, I convinced him that we could do more scouting with our binoculars than on foot. We sat at our vantage point until 4 p.m., when Jim became restless and set off again.

"Damn it!" he swore. "Whoever made this map ought to be put in jail for misrepresentation. Not one elk in the whole country!"

After that outburst I didn't catch up with him until I reached the camp again. He was stowing his gear in the car and getting ready to leave, while talking with two newly arrived hunters. I overheard Jim's,"...there are no elk in this neck of the woods."

One of the hunters, a young Italian, was short, swarthy and obviously impulsive.

"Baloney! I've been here before." His arms gestured as if to show us herds of elk. "I shot lotsa elk here."

"You did what?" Jim dropped his suitcase on the ground and pumped for more information. "How did you find 'em, I mean, where the hell are they?"

"Right here. If you guys want, I'll show you in the morning? You'll see."

Of course, Jim wanted to see. Right off he figured he had himself a free guiding service.

"Did you hear what that fellow said?" he asked as we lay wrapped in our bedrolls. "Twenty elk he's shot in this neighbourhood."

"Yeah," I replied. Actually, the Italian fellow somehow hadn't impressed me. I had done a few quick calculations — dividing the fellow's age by the number of hunting seasons required to kill that many elk—and it seemed he must've shot his first at five years of age when he still lived in sunny Napoli. His partner, though, a husky Dane, seemed like a straight, nice fellow. However, as long as they could keep Jim in the area I was happy enough.

"We'll see about that in the morning," I said.

Jim was awfully excited about the Italian's story. All night long he tossed and rolled about, shaking the double bunk. Then, when the patter of a packrat's feet bothered me, and I reached for my .22, Jim grabbed my arm.

"Let 'er be," he yawned. "It's 5 a.m.; we've got to get up anyway."

He rose at once. I lingered for another couple of winks while he stepped outside. The Italian and his partner were still asleep in another shack and they were not pleased at being roused this early. I could hear an angry bellow directed at Jim. It was nearly 9 a.m. before the Italian finally led us off on the zigzagging trail we already knew. He and Jim had filled their pockets with food and vowed not to return without an elk apiece. The Dane only smiled through all the talk and blinked an eye occasionally. I had signaled back to him.

The mountain seemed twice as high as on the previous day.

It was well past my lunch time before we reached the basin again.

"No stopping here," said the Italian. "Too early. We go!" "Hold it a minute!" the Dane fairly shouted, and mimicking his partner's delightful accent, "Not-a mia!" "And not-a mia, either," I echoed.

"Oh, come on you guys, what's the matter?"

"Okay," the Dane replied, "I'll tell you. Supposing you do find an elk up there—how do you get him out?" He looked at me, blinked his eye quickly and explained that he wasn't about to rupture himself packing a bull elk off the top of a 9,000-foot high mountain. "Don't let me hold you back, though. Come four o'clock I mean to wander home again —to the camp, you know. If you want my help with your elk, you had better bring him back here by four; otherwise look after yourselves."

"Yeah, I'll subscribe to that," I said, and added: "If you shoot something, build a smoky signal fire right away so we can see it, then we'll wait an extra hour. How's that?"

The boys didn't appreciate our attitude, but finally agreed to the proposal. The Dane just shook his head and grumbled. "Nuts!"

At 3 p.m. it sounded like a shooting war had broken out between them. Thirteen shots echoed around the basin like thunder. The Dane and I searched for even the faintest wisp of a signal smoke. At four he shook his head sadly.

"They missed whatever it was they shot at. Maybe a mean old grizzly is eating 'em now for an afternoon snack." Together we speculated on the cause for the shooting. We had looked at every rock, tree and bush in the basin without seeing any sign of our partners.

"Let's go home," the Dane continued, "Let them spend the night up here."

It was dark when we reached our cabins. It felt good to walk right in, start a fire in the stove and cook supper. It felt good too, to share all this with the Dane. He was a man after my own heart. On our way off the mountain he had told me that hunting for the sole purpose of killing was meaningless to him. He had come to this country hoping to take a good trophy, but even more than that he wanted to enjoy the out doors, and the comradeship that went with hunting.

We sat up long past our normal bedtime, talking. We drank countless cups of coffee and discussed our partners, agreeing that from now on we would be awfully choosey about whom we hunted with. "I was only kidding before," he said. "I don't want them to get hurt by any old bear. And they did mean to stay overnight — didn't they?

By midnight we switched from coffee to wine. The Italian had brought three gallon-sized jugs and the Dane figured we were entitled to at least one.

"It serves him right," he stated, "for leaving it unprotected. Besides, with all the worrying over him I think we deserve something."

The stuff was sour as vinegar but potent. I didn't like it at first, but the Dane — seeing my grimace — poured in a generous quantity of sugar and heated it on the stove. Suddenly it became drinkable. I reckon our consciences did bother us somewhat, because we drank many a toast to the boy's health. Our stove roared, the night deepened and soon we were at peace with the world.

It was early morning — 3 or 4 a.m. — when stumbling footsteps interrupted our pleasant conversation. I grabbed the lantern and opened the door. My heart missed a few beats when I saw Jim. The Italian was right behind him and both were covered with grime and blood. My first thought was that a grizzly had wiped the trail with them. They stumbled into the cabin and plunked themselves down by the stove. They seemed exhausted but unhurt.

The Dane recovered his speech first. "For goodness sake, what happened to you?"

The answer came after a long burst of mixed English and Italian profanity. They had run into a herd of elk, the Italian explained, and he had uncorked a few shells at them. Jim, not to be outdone, had followed his example. All this was fine, Jim allowed, except for the fact that the "elk" turned out to be large mule deer bucks.

"No, no, no!" The Italian still swore they were elk and told us they had argued over this and over which trophy belonged to each hunter. In fact, he and Jim still weren't on the best of terms.

Anyhow, when they finally and duly recognized each other's claims and made a signal fire, it was too late for us to see it.

"We wanted to bring 'em out whole," Jim explained. "We dragged 'em for a while but it was too rough a job. We had to butcher them. We hoisted the hindquarters and antlers of each buck onto our shoulders-and that's it. It was one hell of a load. Look at all that blood." He took off his coat and showed us that even his shirt was drenched.

The Italian was still labouring for each breath, but he interrupted again, insisting the game was elk and gasping about "a bear in the bush."

"Yeah,"grunted Jim. " There was one hell of a roar right in front of us. We couldn't see him, but it was a bear alright; I could smell his foul breath. We stopped dead in our tracks. I mean, we had our hands full of venison, rifles on our backs - if we had dropped the meat I don't think we could've lifted it back up again. So I just hollered at the beast, told him to beat it. It worked. I don't know how long it took — seemed like hours but then we heard the bushes crackle as he moved off. We just talked awfully loud after that and hoped he'd stay away."

The Dane had gone outside to inspect the venison and trophies. He came in again and interrupted the Italian's enthusiastic comments about their success. "If a conservation officer checks those hindquarters he'll confiscate them and pinch you guys to boot. You might as well have given it all to the bear."

Jim had his mouth open wide in protest but the Dane wasn't finished.

"You removed all evidence of sex from the carcasses. Why? It's against the law - you've got to leave evidence attached. Either the horns or the sex organs."

Jim insisted that no so-and-so game warden was going to take his game away: "Over my dead body."

Even though the hour was late and the boys were tuckered out, all of us argued the finer points of British Columbia's game laws and discussed acceptable hunting practices for some time - albeit without convincing Jim that all his effort had been for naught.

The Dane had more immediate success with his partner. Mind you, he created fairly realistic scenes of gloomy jail cells, stern judges and clanging steel bars; he scared the Italian so much that he agreed that night to abandon his venison. Checking and rechecking the hunting regulations, I couldn't find a legal way to take Jim's portion home.

"Just take the antlers," I said to him, "put your tag on them and you're okay; that's the prescribed method." Finally, Jim agreed.

The others left for home around noon the next day and suddenly Jim prepared for departure too. He collected his gear, left his venison hanging in the shade of the cabin and said good-bye.

"I'll come back to fetch you home in four days," were his last words.

The camp became suddenly quiet. Too

quiet, really, for I had enjoyed the Dane's company; but presently it felt good not to have arguments and commotion. For the next three days I hunted with little success. I saw a number of deer I might've shot, but there were no elk to be found. One bear came into camp at night trying to get the venison; I chased him away and moved the meat into my cabin so it was handy for cutting my breakfast and dinner steaks.

On the evening before Jim was due back I had just heated my frying pan and dropped in a large steak when the door opened and a tall uniformed conservation officer asked if he could come in.

"Please do," I replied. "Supper's about ready, grab yourself a plate from the shelf and sit down."

"Steak, huh? Sure smells good. What is it, deer, elk?"

"Mule deer," I replied.

"You got one then, huh?"

"No. Some other guys shot it and left it here." "Is that so?"

Suspicious by virtue of his occupation, the officer asked a lot of questions. I was hard pressed to answer promptly and accurately. He didn't eat the supper I set before him but quizzed me constantly until I became annoyed. I had only eaten half of my steak when he suddenly asked to see my licence and tags.

"Right now?" I asked. "Right now." he echoed.

"Well, you can damn well wait until I finish my supper. Right?"

"Wrong!" he growled.

I showed him my license, the elk tag and finally the hindquarters of Jim's buck. He looked at everything carefully and announced that I would have to go with him.

"But my partner's due back anytime now - I've got to stay here."

"Maybe so. And maybe not. I'll have to check your story out and then, maybe, I'll bring you back here. Pack your stuff in my truck and come along. Yes, the meat too. Hurry up."

I can't repeat here the language I used, but I told him that I would take it up with his boss just as soon as I could get back to Vancouver. "You'll be sorry!" I threatened.

He did little talking after that, which was a relief to me. He helped me pack and drove me to the nearest police station where he talked privately with a sergeant who just nodded, looked awfully mean, and before I knew how it happened put me inside a jail cell.

As he locked the door the sergeant grinned. "Confidentially," he asked, "Why did you make that man mad at you? He's usually a real nice fellow. But never tell him you'll complain to his boss about him. That's stupidity."

After he'd left I sat on the jail bunk; only one dim light illuminated my unusual surroundings. I was so mad at the world I could've screamed, and it was this righteous anger within that kept me up, pacing the small cell until a constable brought my breakfast. I didn't eat it. Shortly before 10 a.m. the constable came to lead me into a small courtroom. I meant to give the magistrate an earful; the constable must've guessed my intentions.

"Take it easy now," he urged. "Be very polite and objective, perhaps he'll let you off easy."

Of course, without Jim, or the Dane and Italian, I couldn't prove my innocence. I would have gladly faced ten angry bears instead of that courtroom.

When the magistrate arrived I quickly stepped forward; the constable pulled me back and told me to sit and wait my turn.

A couple of bruised and shabby looking individuals were called up first. They had been drunk, started a fight and wrecked the town's beer parlour the previous night. Both pleaded guilty and were sentenced to 30 days in jail. I shuddered, remembering my own sleepless night.

Next up was a speeding charge against a young motorist who pled not guilty but found himself paying a $25 fine. I winced at that verdict.

The third case was against a fellow who had killed a cow elk out of season. The very same conservation officer came forward to zealously prosecute this case. The magistrate ordered a $350 fine and the seizure of all equipment-car, gun, etc— used in the crime. Furthermore... if the fellow couldn't pay — three months in jail. I nearly fainted.

Then it was my turn. A charge of illegal possession of game was read to the court. The game warden didn't spare one single detail. When someone asked for my full name I couldn't even speak; my throat felt dry and I nearly swallowed my tonsils. My heart pounded my previous anger to pieces. Then I blurted out the whole story. No one interrupted. After that I just stood there on wobbly legs not knowing what to do next.

A smile crept over the magistrate's face. I thought he looked malicious. He peered over his reading glasses and spoke.

"Young man, I am inclined to believe your story. However, you were found in sole possession of game without a corresponding cancelled tag licence. Further, you were unable to provide satisfactory evidence of sex on the carcass. Therefore, I must sentence you." He paused, looking as stern as a prison wall.

My knees buckled, my head vibrated like a beehive.

"The minimum fine is $13. Do you wish to pay this amount to the court clerk?" He began to say that the alternative would be a three-day jail sentence, but I interrupted him.

"I'll pay! Oh, yes, Sir!" I gasped. Then, with my wallet in my hands, "Right away, Sir."

"All right then, court's adjourned."

Finally, outside the building, drinking in the

sweet air of freedom, I was grabbed by the shoulder. I just about zoomed out of my boots and then I heard Jim's hysterical laughter. "Man, you handled that just great," he laughed. "Couldn't have done better myself!"

"Where the hell did you come from?" I sputtered, perplexed and annoyed. "You were in there?"

"Yeaaaah!" Laughter shook him so hard that he sounded like a billy goat. "I just drove in this morning to report you missing. The police sergeant told me you were in court. Well done. But tell me, why did you keep that meat around the cabin after you told me it was so hell-fired illegal?"

"It just seemed like a damn shame to waste it, you know. And, by the way, you owe me thirteen bucks."

1959

Five species of grouse inhabit the forest and grasslands of B.C. and often provide excellent hunting. Usually, though, grouse are taken when hunters are out after larger game, and are considered a sort of booby prize.

The spruce grouse (or foolhens, as they are commonly called), actually consist of two species — the Franklin and Hudsonion. They appear to be quite tame and are often taken with little more than a slingshot or a stick. The blue and ruffed grouse species are probably the most difficult to approach and hunt. The sharp-tailed grouse is a bird of grasslands and sub-alpine forests and meadows. In peak cycle years, grouse provide much excitement for hunters and some excellent meals for the table. They probably deserve more respect and attention from hunters than they get.

Chapter 4:

Grouse: The Best Booby Prize

"Hey! Wait a minute! Stop! Hold it, will you!" Joe Ringwald sputtered like an irate general before he finally explained:

"There's a whole flock of grouse sitting on the road just ahead."

"Where?" Wayne Place asked.

"Right around the next bend," Joe replied. "I saw them as we came around the switchback from the river."

I hadn't seen any birds, but I was driving and the bad road had commanded all of my attention. On our left, 50 feet down the steep gravel bank, flowed the glacier-blue waters of the Kootenay River; and on our right, towards the summit of the Rocky Mountains, rose an evergreen parkland of pine, spruce and tamarack.

Neither Joe or Wayne had planned to hunt grouse with me on this gorgeous October morning; we had come all of the 700-odd miles from Vancouver in hopes that an early snowstorm might have driven some elk and deer off the high ranges. But instead the sun was out, fresh dew sparkled on grasses and shrubs among the trees. There wasn't a cloud to mar the sky. We had listened to the weather report while breakfasting in Canal Flats and the weatherman had promised more Indian summer for the week ahead.

It was Wayne who had suggested a drive up the Kootenay Valley anyway; he had overheard some talk of fabulous grouse shooting there. "And besides," he had added, "you never can tell - we might run into some stray elk after all. Sure hope that weatherman's all wrong this time."

"Yeah," Joe had interrupted. "It seems I recollect some talk of this being a peak year for grouse. Why do you think we've got our shotguns along? Why not hunt them properly for a change?" Joe talked himself into a real enthusiasm. "You know, grouse hunting can be just as exciting as stalking elk."

We had hoped to do a little pothole duck hunting on our way home, thus our guns were 12 gauge. Wayne had a fine Ithaca pump gun, which he presently unwrapped. Joe and I had side-by-side doubles, bored full and modified chokes which, as we had previously learned, patterned awfully tight for upland birds.

I couldn't help pondering the possibilities, but Joe, handing me a box of #6s grinned and remarked that these loads might be a little rough on grouse. "Suppose we'll have to give 'em a good head start, 40 yards or so or we'll have an awful lot of lead filling in our hollow teeth tonight."

Wayne was the first to slip out of the car. "Let's get all the guns loaded first," he suggested, "and then walk up to 'em slowly."

It was a typical grouse situation, eight birds sat right on the road, some dusting themselves in the fine powdery clay and others, seemingly finished with their morning toilet, pecked the fine gravel they must eat to properly digest their food.

Guns at the ready, we walked abreast to within 40 yards and waited for the birds to fly off. Five minutes later Wayne urged us to resume the stalk. Thirty yards, twenty, still nothing happened; at ten paces the spruce and Franklin's sat unconcerned. Only occasionally an odd bird craned its neck to look at us, making us feel rather over-armed and foolish.

"Listen you fools!" Joe shouted. "Don't just sit there-fly!" He kicked a pebble at them but the birds sat tight.

"What's next?" I asked. "Can't shoot 'em at this range with our "Big Bertha's"; we'll blow 'em to bits. Should we back off again?"

Wayne picked up a rock and tossed it at a fat strutting cock Franklin. He missed and the bird ignored him. Another stone hurled and another miss. These grouse couldn't be bothered to fly.

"I'd sure like to know what proper grouse hunting's supposed to look like," Wayne joked.

"It seems to me all the grouse that I ever hunted just got their heads clipped off with a well aimed bullet. Would have felt sorry for 'em— except I love to eat 'em. Maybe I'd better get the little .22 from the car."

Before Wayne finished talking I heaved a dry branch boomerang-fashion. That did it. The whole bunch flew - straight up to perch in the nearest tree.

Joe shook his head and laughed. "I guess we can't win our supper this-a-way ... Just stick around another minute." He joked, and ran back to the car to fetch the little rifle that I always carry for just this purpose.

The small bullet drilled into the foolish cock's head and he fell to the road. Another bird flew off and Wayne's shotgun brought it down. But the rest still perched, although they were somewhat confused by now.

While I reloaded the rifle Joe thought out loud: "This feels like an execution to me. It's too bad they aren't willows or blues - they don't behave this stupidly. A fellow needs a shotgun for 'em and plenty of hitting luck to boot. I guess that's why it's called sport."

I shared Joe's sentiments completely, but knew it was either "execute" or go without supper. With the second crack of the little rifle another cock fell. Then, suddenly, the air was full of buzzing wings beating away from the scene. Both Joe's and Wayne's hasty shots missed completely. "Hey, who said they can't fly," Wayne remarked dryly. That's the way it is with grouse. I have learned that at times you can knock the smartest old willow hen off her roost with a pole, but usually, they'll flush 100 yards ahead of the finest pointing dog so that you never get a sporting shot away.

I don't remember my very first grouse-for one thing it was too long ago and for another it must've been an insignificant hunt - but there was one season I won't ever forget. It was 1957, on Bromley Mountain near Princeton, when I saw hundreds of grouse during a two-week elk hunt on horseback.

On my first morning out, riding a big clumsy gelding along a hillside, I must've been daydreaming. Suddenly, as horses will do on occasion, the gelding shied and broke away down hill: leaving me sitting in the air while a large covey of blue grouse thundered through the jack pines.

Every single night of that hunt I had grouse for supper, every day I shot one of them. I didn't do it out of revenge either, they just tasted too good to pass up. I fried them in a covered pot, adding butter, a couple of slices of bacon, a small onion, some salt and pepper. In 35 minutes they were cooked in their own delicious juices. Since those days, I might add, I've also learned not to trust strange horses in grouse country.

My hunting partner, Frank Kasa, rode with me on another morning along that very same trail. I wasn't riding the clumsy gelding then. Frank was riding 20 paces ahead when I saw a brace of foolhens sitting right on the trail. Frank was occupied searching for deer and I made a bet with myself about how high his horse would buck if spooked by grouse.

I hate to admit it, but I was downright disappointed when Frank's horse, stepping high, walked carefully over the birds. You must understand that I didn't mean Frank any harm, I like the guy very much, but I did wonder how a weekend horseman would handle his mount "walking on wings" so to speak.

I have also often wondered how some territory can be good for grouse, while in previous seasons it held no birds at all. It seems as though grouse populate ranges in cycles, not unlike lemmings or snowshoe hares. Perhaps the best explanation for this phenomenon comes from biologists and conservation officers that I know, who report that weather conditions during mating and nesting season are most likely to influence survival rates of the young chicks and are indeed the only logical explanation.

"If you look at an area that's been hit by severe weather," one conservation officer told me, "and the grouse have been nearly wiped out because of it, you only find good hunting there again after a few favourable seasons."

This would seem to explain fluctuations in rabbit population as well. I have made a number of trips north along the Alaska Highway to Whitehorse without ever seeing a single grouse or rabbit on the road. One of my partners on these trips used to get mad about that.

"Darn it all," he used to mutter. "A fellow can find more moose on this road than grouse and rabbits!" Then on a trip during the 1970 season we found conditions had changed dramatically; my friend had little reason to complain. We counted hundreds of the big-footed bunnies and a fair number of grouse, particularly near Mile 219, between Trutch, B.C. and Fort Nelson. The countryside crawled with rabbits. But again we found long stretches of barren country as well. It's a regional cycle too, it seems.

I have mentioned these peculiarities only because you too might have pondered the boom or bust cycles of game populations. We know rabbits become completely infested with vermin that help distribute disease until an epidemic wipes out whole populations. I have heard that grouse may be subject to a similar fate.

Only a year ago, Frank Kasa and I blundered into many flocks of blue grouse while searching for California bighorns on Crater Mountain near Keremeos. I didn't trust my eyes when these birds proved to be as tame as foolhens. Clucking and calling to each other, but still feeding in a wild rose bush, they let us walk up to within a few feet. We shot two birds with our rifles before the rest flushed. After we retrieved our prize Frank said, "Are you sure they're blues? They looked like foolhens to me. Acted like 'em anyway."

They were all young birds and if it hadn't been for their yellow eye patches I too might've mistaken them for spruce grouse. Of course there are other identification marks. Normally an adult blue is much larger than the average foolhen. The tip of the blue's tail is grey. Whereas the tail is a rusty or yellow ochre colour in spruce grouse, and black like the rest of the tail in Franklin's grouse – yet the two species commonly referred to as foolhens.

Under certain conditions it is quite possible to make a mistake, especially if you haven't seen grouse for a number of years or when blues display such uncharacteristic behaviour.

My experience has suggested that blues are the wildest of our grouse, next to the ruffed or willow, and on many occasions have proven impossible to approach. On one warm September day in 1967 I was riding around the Twin Buttes near the B.C.-Washington border, hunting for deer, when I flushed a covey of large blues right into the U.S. - or so it seemed, without getting a single bird for the pot.

In conclusion, I'm sorry to say that most of us— myself included— all too often regard a grouse as some sort of booby prize, to be taken when larger game eludes us. Just like that day on the Kootenay River when we had elk in mind, or on other occasions when sheep and deer have been the object. But be it ruffed, blue, foolhen or sharp-tailed, many a beautiful bird hits the dust with its head clipped off by powerful bullets that were meant for much larger game.

Government records show that during the 1968 season 978,485 birds were killed. The actual kill was probably much greater. But, as my friend Pat Wright might say, "Booby prize or not, in anybody's yard, them's an awful lot o' chickens." And to a hungry hunter each grouse is a very fine chicken indeed.

1964

When Papa visited me and my family in 1964, he had not seen us since I had immigrated to Canada 12 years before. I had written to him about my many hunting adventures, and he badly wanted to hunt in Canada. The hunting trip described here was the total reverse of the traditional father and son hunting trip and is an experience I will never forget. Papa loved British Columbia, and it was on his advice that I finally became a Canadian citizen.

Chapter 5:

A Bear for Papa

The morning of April 2, 1964 was rainy and wet in Vancouver. Heavy drops hammered onto the gleaming tarmac of the Sea Island airport and the day promised to remain dark and dreary. Since 3 a.m. my family and I had been waiting for the CP Air flight from Montreal that was to bring my dear old father for a visit. Finally, at 6:45 a.m. the plane stood outside the terminal and passengers began streaming into the building. Our excitement mounted from minute to minute. Alas, Papa did not appear.

Knowing the old man, I should have guessed that Herr Heinrich Prante senior, retired factory manager and alderman of the town of Sehnde, in the county of Burgdorf, West Germany, would surely be the last to arrive. He never did like to shove and push his way to the front.

Impatiently, we continued to wait. "What will he look like?" we pondered. I had not seen him in a dozen years and my children did not know him at all. They only knew their grandfather was supposed to come any moment and would no doubt bring presents and candy. They also knew the old man wanted to hunt a bear.

Then the crew left the plane and we began to despair. Suddenly one last passenger appeared in the doorway, came down the ramp and started across the tarmac. A flight attendant, who must have guessed that we were waiting for this last passenger, whispered to me that the old man had wanted to compose himself before disembarking.

When he embraced us, however, all that composure melted away like winter snow in a Chinook wind.

After Papa had wiped the liquid joy off his face and we got into my car, he said suddenly, "Where in hell are all your bears? You wrote to me that you have an abundance of them in Canada. Why haven't I seen one yet?"

I was glad that Papa had not lost his sense of humour, but in the bright light of the airport terminal I had noticed the deep lines in his face. Could I really expect him to go bear hunting? He looked so fragile. Of course, he had to be dead tired from the long flight that originated in Hannover.

After a brief time with us, Papa felt acclimatized enough to go hunting. He inspected my arsenal and polished guns. On each Sunday drive into the country he asked if we should take a hunting rifle along. It was not easy to convince him that a spring bear hunt was not going to be as easy as he had, perhaps, imagined.

"There are bears everywhere," he was told by some of my friends and acquaintances who took delight in worsening the old man's already bad case of "bear-fever." Of course, only a few of those folks realized that before the middle of May bears are hard to find indeed.

During our month of waiting I gathered information and tried to learn which part of the province held bears that would be out of hibernation. Finally, my old friend Maximilian Winkler told me that bears had been seen feeding in some mountain meadows in the Bridge River area.

"And maybe," he added, "the road to McGillvray Pass will be open. There are supposed to be plenty of bears in that country."

This was interesting news because I knew the area from previous hunting trips. If the snows were gone already it would be good bear habitat indeed. Also, I knew that we could stay with friends in Gold Bridge or Bralorne if we chose to go there. I was pleased when Dan Bowers — a friend originally from Toronto-asked to go with us. He would get to see some new territory and provide our party with a handy extra rifle.

The day was fine and warm when we left Vancouver. My station wagon was crammed full: I knew that our journey would take us into some pretty high country and we could not afford to skimp on gear and provisions. Papa, gentleman that he was, had even washed the car before we left. On top of our load lay Papa's Bergstock, a stout cane with a stag handle. "How far is it to this city of Gold Bridge?" Papa asked us.

Since Dan could not speak or understand our native German and Papa spoke no English, I answered this question and acted as translator on our trip.

"It's about 600 miles or 1,000 kilometres."
"What? One way?" Papa was impressed.

"The round trip," I said, hoping Papa's imagination would not run away with him. He was still not used to Canadian geography and either greatly under- or over-estimated distances. In Germany, a 1000-kilometre drive would be considered a major undertaking.

Papa was confused when I explained that the road ahead was a "dead" end. Only when I translated a sign proudly proclaiming that hundreds of millions of dollars in gold had been mined in that area did he comprehend that one could afford to hack and blast a road into the wilderness and let it stop just anywhere.

Bralorne was almost a ghost town in that spring of 1964. Its only hotel was nearly deserted as we stopped in to have lunch and wash off the dust of the road. In the dining room we were pleased to find my old friend Otto Kapillari. We had looked for him at his cabin in Gold Bridge, but a note on his door said that he would be in Bralorne for the day.

Otto was Austrian and had come to the Gold Bridge area directly from his native Styria and worked as a painter. He knew the area well and I had hoped he might hunt with us.

Otto had guessed the reason for our arrival. "Sure the bears are out now. Up the Cadwallader River—towards McGillvray. But just imagine, fellows, I can't go with you, I've got to work! It's a hard sentence on a day like this, eh? Well, you don't need me anyway. You know your way around here by now, don't you? Tonight you all came back to my place and tell me about your hunting, you hear?" While our conversation with Otto was brief, it was as warm as usual. Great Styrian hospitality embraced me whenever I hunted in Otto's neighbourhood. He accepted Papa and Dan as long-lost friends.

Heinrich," he said in his native tongue with a smattering of high German intertwined, "don't let these kids tie a bear to your tail. And make damn sure you don't get eaten by one of those bruins either. They are hungry now, you know." Otto was closer to Papa in age and knew he could afford to joke at my expense. "Actually it is a little late in the day to go to the pass. Why don't you drive over to Green Mountain. A few days ago a boy I know saw a big grizzly over there on the flats." His hand indicated that the bear had had a shoulder height of five feet. "The fellow only had a little 30-30 carbine and was too scared to start a war with a big grizzly."

Papa looked somewhat puzzled and Otto noticed it. "Are you scared, Heinrich?" he asked.

"No, I wouldn't be here if I were scared, but that big? Who is trying to fool me now, please?" Papa had seen some bears in Stanley Park and obviously doubted Otto's tale.

We laughed and after lunch took the road to Green Mountain, a massive, snow-covered ridge across the deep Cadwallader canyon. The road was barely passable. Since the mines were closed and timber wasn't being cut no one looked after the roads. Even the old Hurley River bridge had collapsed and lay in the river. Other sections of road were washed out or covered with rocks. We did not get far before we had to leave the wagon behind and hunt on foot.

The afternoon sun burned with unseasonal heat. Spring melt water bubbled and gurgled in streams and crevasses, but along the road the ground was baked dry. There were few tracks. No birds fluttered about. No squirrels foraged in this heat. No moose or deer or bear moved about - only bumblebees and flies buzzed through the sweet-scented spring air. The whole plateau seemed barren of life. We hiked slowly and soon found a path that led past a rotting old cabin towards the tree line.

Then, in the baked mud of a dry puddle, we found a bear's footprint - the calling card of a grizzly. The imprints of his toenails were as long as our fingers. It was at least two days old, I guessed, and would lead us upwards on that steeply rising trail.

I looked at Papa and wondered if he could still make the climb. The bear had probably gone all the way up and was now hunting for marmots on a. south slope or in a snow-free meadow. It would be too far for the old man. So, even though Papa was very excited about the find and wanted to follow that bear, I called off the hunt. We would try for something less strenuous on another day.

At first light the next day we set out again. The sky was still clear. The day promised more heat. Through thick layers of dust we drove to Bralorne again and beyond. Finally a mile past Pioneer Mine the road became impassable. Brush grew up everywhere and in the shade of tall trees the snow was too deep for the car. I knew the area from a previous hunt when a friend collected a beautiful bear rug. It would be a six-mile hike to the foot of the pass, but it was reasonably level going. I hoped that Papa would get his bear long before we reached the pass.

The snow on sky-scraping mountains fed the many rivulets that cascaded into nearby Cadwallader River. The air was full of the sounds of singing water and tender new grass grew everywhere near the trail of sandy soil. Ruffed grouse celebrated the final arrival of spring with noisy courtship dances.

The peculiar sounds caused Papa to stop a few times and listen attentively.

"Is there a farm nearby?" he asked suddenly.

"Out here, in the wilderness? What makes you think that?" I asked.

"Well, all morning long it's sounded like some poor devil was trying to start an old tractor engine. Don't you hear it? Whup-whup-whuppupupupupup, then it quits again!"

"Oh, that- those are grouse, wild chicken, they look like the German Haselhuhn. They make that noise with their wings to impress the women of their tribe."

"You may be right," Papa allowed after giving the subject some thought. "But it still reminds me of some cranky old tractor engine."

We laughed and when I translated Papa's remarks to Dan he agreed. "When I was a kid on the farm in Ontario we had a tractor that sounded just like that."

Suddenly, Papa forgot about tractors as he spotted a bear track in the moist sand of the road. Not a grizzly but a black bear had left its big and distinct track on the trail. With Papa in the lead we began to hunt seriously.

Because of all the rushing water in the vicinity and the bush on either side of the trail we could not trust our ears too much. "It wouldn't do to surprise an angry bear," I thought.

In some places the track was so fresh that water had not seeped in yet. Still, after every bend in the trail we found only the same beautiful but empty landscape.

At noon I called for a halt. Although we had hunted slowly I could see that Papa was a little tired. A good lunch - some soup, bread with back bacon and a cup of coffee- would do us all good.

Dan made a small cooking fire and our pots soon blackened over it. To appease Papa I told him that during the siesta time in the heat of the day no intelligent bear would be seen wandering about.

Papa's patience lasted until 2 p.m., when he suddenly grabbed his rifle and Bergstock and continued to follow the trail of Mr. Bruin, alone. That would not do, so Dan and I packed up in a hurry and followed Papa.

Actually, I was surprised that the same bear had travelled the road for so long. We could still see the scratch marks his claws had left. In water puddles where he had stepped, little clouds of fine silt still hung suspended and showed that Blackie was not too far ahead of us. We saw that he had fed on dandelion stems. After eating the tender, hollow stalks he had spit out the petals. These lay in bunches in the dirt; even the saliva on the petals was wet and fresh.

Then the road led a little uphill and we closed in on Papa- and the bear, we hoped. On our left the forest opened up a little and a slide came into view. Some rocks were on the road and water flowed along the trail as well. With field glasses I searched the slide for tell-tale movements and black shadows. I noticed the shadows of the trees had grown longer and I began to think that we would have to stay out overnight.

We could camp in a ski cabin that belonged to Paul Kleinschrot of Bralorne, who in the previous summer had been mauled by a grizzly in the pass area. I knew where the cabin was because I had stayed there when helping Paul's son look for some of his dad's belongings, lost during the attack. We had hunted for that mean bear too, but had found nothing.

Dan interrupted my thoughts. "It's almost three o'clock now. If that bear wants to be found, he'd better do it soon." I agreed.

We had just stumbled over a small rock pile and were looking for a safe place to set our feet, when we heard Papa, who was still a few steps ahead of us.

"There he is!" The loud report of the 30-06 followed Papa's words.

The old man's shot startled us. About 20 paces in front I saw something black and shiny spin about on the trail, fly through the air over a tall boulder and vanish into a thick willow patch. It was impossible to positively identify a particular shape in that one swift motion, but it had to be a bear. On the road red blotches marred the white sandy soil. Papa must have found the bear feeding on the road and hit him hard— very hard indeed. Papa's gun was a sure bear stopper.

The drama was over. Or was it really? Since I had not seen precisely what had happened and did not know how large or how badly hurt the bear was, I intended to proceed with great caution. For all I knew it could have been a black grizzly. And it could still be alive.

When my gaze returned to Papa he had already shouldered his rifle and with his Bergstock was pointing at the willow patch and the rock splattered with blood.

"In the bush there, that's where he is! I'll go get him!" He had waited a lifetime for this moment and knew no caution. I had to hold him back.

"Ja, was ist los? What's up?" he asked, angered. "That bear is dead! We don't want him to rot!"

"No, Papa. But first we wait a while before we go into that jungle. Sit down. Smoke your pipe. Then, in about twenty minutes or so, when your bear has had time to die gracefully, then Dan and I will go and find him for you. In this bush it isn't easy to find anything. And besides, too many 'dead' bears have mauled careless hunters before. We wait!"

When I explained my plan, Dan agreed. Then Papa and I smoked our pipes. The time passed much too slowly for the old man. He said nothing and puffed quickly on his pipe, as if to hurry everything up.

Finally, the moment of truth arrived. There had been no sounds from the bear, but Dan and I still rechecked our guns and flicked the safety catches off before we moved in. We posted Papa out of the way, in a place where he would have time to react if he needed it. Then we approached the thicket from two directions.

The willows were partially flattened by generations of avalanches and the thicket contained dry wood that crackled under foot. It was no comfort to think that the bear might still be alive and ready to swipe at us. We would not get much notice of his intentions, since we would only see him when we were two or three steps away.

We had searched carefully for about 20 yards when I spotted the animal and heard a low growl that sent shivers up my spine. The great creature looked at me. He was down, but his eyes still watched me. I aimed the double and called for Dan.

I stood perfectly still until Dan arrived. Then I saw the bear's eyes glaze over. He was dead. No second shot was needed.

Now Papa arrived on the scene. He had been quite right when he claimed the bear was dead after his shot. It was hit low in the chest behind the right shoulder. Judging by the bullet's exit hole I concluded that the heart was destroyed. It was only the animal's reflexes that had carried him that far into the bush. Papa had made a great shot, a shot any hunter could be proud of. Together we dragged the bear to the road.

A child's Christmas joy could not have compared with Papa's. With dewy eyes he accepted our congratulations. Again and again he stroked the silky fur. I guessed the bear's weight at 330 pounds.

But Papa still stood as if in a trance or prayer. He had removed his hat and folded his hands. Finally, after some long moments of silence, Dan gently reminded us of the long way home. But Papa just broke out his pipe again and loaded it with tobacco. He lit it.

"We wait!" he said firmly. "Twenty minutes!" Then he sat down on a log and enjoyed his smoke. What could we do but join him?

"Just look at him," he said after a few minutes of silent puffing, "such a fine, silky fur. And look at the claws. What did I tell you — black bear claws! And the mouth—what great teeth! How strong he must have been! He is one majestic beast. I doubt there has never been another bear such as this!"

In the end we had to hurry with the skinning job. We loaded all our gear on three pack boards now. Dan made his back sore taking the hindquarters -which, at the time, he did not know weighed over 100 pounds.

I took the great pelt and Papa carried the leftovers from lunch and our utensils. We had to stop often to rest, but late that night we got back to an anxious Otto, who had his beer cold and his bottle of brandy at the appropriate temperature — both waiting for us.

After an excellent supper we honored an ancient German tradition and drank a few toasts to the departed spirit of the bear. Never has a Canadian been so wonderfully celebrated. It was noon the next day before we were in any condition to begin the long drive home. Seldom have I seen dear old Papa so happy.

Seldom was I so happy. I sure missed him when he returned to Germany.

1967

Not too often have I been impressed with the quality of partnership: the ability and knowledge my late friend Maximilian Winkler possessed. Since our Tatlayoko adventure I have been on many hunts, none, however, were more enjoyable or more successful than the one described here. Max had a special talent for organization and his friendly, outgoing personality was easy to live within the cold climates of a late-season Chilcotin hunt. I miss him these days.

Chapter 6:
Tatlayoko Lake Deer Hunt

We can't just grab ole Betsy off the peg and rush off into the hills hoping we'll find some prime beasts to kill. My time and money's too short- too precious for that. A good hunt, like any recipe, needs some planning and figuring, especially if a fellow wants to play it safe and recreate himself at the same time. I have a plan —you might call it a recipe — for rustling the Tatlayoko deer herd. Well, a few head of 'em anyway. Want to come?" The late Maximilian Winkler smiled as he spoke and his blue eyes twinkled as he addressed Frank Kasa and me.

This conversation took place in November of 1965, just a few days before Max, Frank Kasa and I set out to fetch home said venison. Let me explain.

Max had heard rumours about a great herd of mule deer that winters about the shores of the wild, picturesque Tatlayoko Lake in British Columbia's Chilcotin country. Now you should know that Max was a patient, meticulous sort of fellow, and that it wasn't exactly simple or easy to track down the source of the rumour and collect the maps on which he, with the aid of red crayons, planned his strategy.

You see, all of Max's requests for permission to use the roads in the area - all private - were denied. And without access to the area, even his best plan seemed hopeless at first.

One return letter suggested that he and his company could shoot plenty of deer elsewhere. I suppose the writer was right, in a way, but "Why should a few people hog all the deer in that area?" Max asked. Finally, after considerable thought and research he announced: "We'll go by truck as far as the government road allows and then we'll take our boats. We won't even need private roads!"

On the eve of our departure, quiet, soft-spoken Frank began to stutter as he attempted to comment on the mountains of gear and equipment Max planned to take along.

"Man - this looks like - like the departure from Egypt. Are we-I mean-do we need all this for a week's hunt?"

"It's alright." Max explained. "We have enough room on the truck. And besides, November in that neck of the jack pine country isn't exactly the time for a picnic, you know." It can rain all week or it can snow. It can get cold too; colder'n the answers I got from those people up there. Forty below maybe."

Max had picked such a late date for the hunt because of what he called "proper timing." The deer would be unbothered by the large numbers of hunters and the early winter snow would drive them down from the hills. "We can pick 'em off as they come a-marching by our camp," said Max.

Remote Tatlayoko Lake seemed the best place to go – not just for its wealth of venison, but because it lies hidden at the end of 500 miles of treacherous, slippery roads, and behind billions of screening jack pines. It's tucked away in the deep folds of impassable mountains, behind locked gates and threatening signs, so to speak. All of this helped to make for a good, undisturbed hunt.

Rain was falling the night we left Max's home in Richmond, B.C. Five hours later when we drove through Spences Bridge on the banks of the Thompson River, the rain had turned into snow. Further north, at 100 Mile House in the Cariboo, a full-scale blizzard had smothered the highway in six inches of drifting snow.

After breakfast in Williams Lake, we turned off onto the Bella Coola Road. It was a rare pleasure to drive through the silent Chilcotin past the small settlement at Riske Creek, past Lee's Corner and Alexis Creek, along the excellent steelhead waters of the Chilcotin River to Redstone. The snow stopped as we rambled on over the crooked, slippery stretch to Tatla Lake, and then south 18 miles to Tatlayoko. It wasn't until 3 p.m. that our boats were launched, loaded and ready for the final run to Max's pre-determined campsite.

Tatlayoko Lake sparkled like diamonds in the afternoon sun. The lake, following an almost straight north-south line between the up-heaved and eroded strata of the Potato Ridge to the east and the jagged Niut Range to the west was jade coloured and placid - temporarily. To the southwest, near the glaciers of Mount Tiedemann and Mount Waddington, a storm was brewing. Max urged haste.

The outboards roared into life and soon the first wavelets splashed against the hulls. Max's boat, with Frank aboard, took the lead in the steadily rising swell. As we passed a sawmill site a worker on shore pointed to us and the storm clouds already overhead; he touched his forehead with a finger. Over the roar of the engines I thought I heard him say, "You guys are nuts!"

Max and Frank turned to me, smiling from under their mummy-like wrappings of scarves and shawls and sweaters.

Then the storm struck. As if the winds had blown the sun from the sky, it grew dark and suddenly very cold. Foam blew off the oncoming rows of whitecaps to freeze where it fell. Ice soon covered our decks and windscreens, stuck to our gear and our clothing. Maybe that fellow at the mill was right.

Max's boat was only visible as a small black dot bouncing on top of its own keel water amidst flying spray. His figure and Frank's were already swallowed up by the darkness.

Three uncomfortable hours had passed when Max finally throttled his engine and scanned the shoreline with his searchlight. My glove was frozen to the control arm of the motor.

"Somewhere around 'here is our beach," he hollered over the driving wind. "Watch out and don't swamp!"

We bounced and sloshed about a small peninsula where the breakers lost some force. I was wearing chest-high waders for loading and unloading the small craft, and as the first gravel scraped the keel I scrambled over the side into knee-deep water. I grabbed the painter and pulled the boat high and dry onto the snow covered beach. Max and Frank followed like clumsy, stiff-legged robots.

Numb fingers lit the gas lanterns and in

their pale flickering light we pitched the tents among gnarled, ghostly looking cottonwoods. Shelter at last. My watch showed 7 p.m. The whole trip had taken exactly 24 hours.

Frank stirred with the first light of dawn. "Max, get up," he called out, "get up and show me where all those deer are."

Max's muffled snoring stopped abruptly. A low grunt escaped from the downy folds of his bedroll.

I was enjoying the warmth and comfort of my bed too much to abandon it easily. It was beastly cold outside. Frank, generous soul and understanding friend that he is, served me breakfast in bed.

"Just you take it easy my good pal," he said and smiled, "because when I shoot my big buck I'll need a strong helper to drag him back here."

Daylight had come to the cottonwood grove when I set out to hunt. Towards the east, through a pass between the high mountains, the sun neared the horizon. The storm had swept the skies clean again and left them a cold steel blue. Across the lake, over the 10,000-foot-high ridges of Razorback Mountain, the winds still raged - rolling the snow into gigantic combers of white, frozen "surf". Tiny, glistening crystals drifted out over the lake.

A flight of snow geese winged down from the north; they talked as they spotted the camp and continued on course for warmer climates. My thermometer read 15°F. The white blanket underfoot was soft and fluffy.

Frank and Max had left early, but not before we had studied the map again. I had noticed the small creek then; it sprang from the bench land above our camp, raced through a narrow canyon and then, its speed decreasing, drifted through the cottonwoods not far from the camp to meet the lake.

"There are supposed to be grizzlies above the canyon," Max had warned. "Better watch out for 'em."

I found the first fresh deer tracks and droppings within a few yards of the tents. It was plain that a whole herd of migrating deer had wandered by during the night. I hunted slowly and carefully and had not gone 100 yards when two shots echoed across the lake; they seemed to have come from the first terrace-like bench. Was it Max's 308 magnum or Frank's 270? Had they found their venison already?

Stopping often, I used my glasses to scan the thickets ahead. When I reached the creek, gushing water drowned out every other sound. The soft shadows of tree and bush fooled the eyes easily in that blue, morning light.

A movement caught my attention. Standing right there in the open was a handsome buck. He was looking towards a willow thicket, while his big ears swivelled and sifted the sounds of the forest. He turned to face me when my careless feet dislodged a rock and it splashed into the creek. His head snapped up in alarm. His alert eyes stared into my scope. I was still 80 yards away, but he recognized danger. His nostrils twitched and he lifted a foot to stamp out the alarm. Then, with the blast of my 30-06, he collapsed.

I reloaded instantly when another, the grand-daddy of all mule deer, walked from the willows as if nothing had happened. Still partly covered by twigs and branches, he scanned the area, sniffing and testing the wisp of a breeze that drifted – luckily – towards me.

He followed a scattering of small, scrubby bushes that led towards the downed buck. He was a huge animal, but his antlers, large as they were, sprouted only two points on the left and three large, unsymmetrical points on the right. His mouth was open as if he intended to bite the dead buck, and it gave him a mean, ornery appearance.

I inched out onto the ice for an unobstructed shot. My cross wires danced excitedly over his muscular, rut-swollen neck. I kneeled on the ice to steady my shaking arms, and then yanked the trigger. The gun bucked against my shoulder, the ice broke and I fell through into waist-deep water.

The whole countryside seemed to explode into movement. Deer bounced and bounded everywhere. I don't know how I'd failed to see them before. The big fellow got away clean; I was disappointed but I did see him again, alas, under different circumstances.

Hurriedly I cleaned my buck and ran back to change my clothes. But back at camp, barely in dry underwear, I was surprised by another deer. Next I heard Max call out to me. He was chasing the deer that had surprised me. When I saw Max he was still a couple of hundred yards away.

"Watch for a deer!" he hollered.

I looked up and saw the doe, obviously wounded, stumbling right by the tent. I had been uncoiling a rope to use as a clothesline. I was ready to drop the line when I glanced at my rifle- it was completely iced up from my dip in the creek. Without thinking I made a loop, lasso fashion, ran after the doe and let the rope fly. Surprise of surprises, the rope caught her by the neck. She pulled and struggled, dragging me on my heel-less moccasins over the snow. Luckily the rope was 100 feet long, so I had enough to tie it around a tree. When the poor beast reached the end of her line she was just belly-deep into the false safety of the lake.

Max stormed into our camp. He hadn't seen my act with the rope. "Where is she? Why didn't you shoot her? I think I've wounded her. We can't let her get away to suffer or die!" Then he saw the twitching rope.

He rubbed his eyes and shook his head, unbelieving. Then he saw my rifle covered with ice leaning against the camp table. With a sigh he lifted his own gun and with one bang the disagreeable, unpleasant job was done. He had guessed right; his first bullet, fired early that morning, had been deflected by brush and ricocheted into the animal's abdomen. It would've been fatal within hours so my rope, cruel as it seemed, actually saved the doe from more agony. Frank came back while Max was cleaning the doe. He had seen a nice buck but missed him.

For the next two days our hunting was reduced to simply selecting rather than searching out game. Deer popped from every other bush and once, on the second morning, another doe walked right through the camp, waking us with loud snorts. It sounded like she was cussing at us. Max said it would be a dirty trick to shoot her and we let her go in peace.

That afternoon Max walked up to and shot two four-point bucks with as many shells - quick, clean kills — and I, having mainly goulash in mind, shot two big, fat does. Frank wasn't quite that lucky; he was still hunting for a trophy, a beast as large as the buck I'd missed. He said he wasn't going to shoot just any old deer.

On our third day I drove Frank to the south shore of the lake, where he promptly found a fair antlered moose. It would've been an easy shot for an air rifle, but Frank shrugged his shoulders."What am I going to do with him?" he asked, "that hull's got a little too much meat for me. He'd fill the whole trunk in a hurry."

On the fourth day the lake stayed calm, so Max and I took advantage of this and ran our game back to the truck while Frank continued his search for a trophy buck. On our return he had a fat doe hanging from a birch tree near the beach.

"I don't like her much," he lamented, "but she'll be better'n no goulash at all. My buck's probably left the country by now."

Finally, our last hunting day dawned. Snow had fallen again during the preceding night and another three inches of clean, new carpet covered all old tracks. Max and I, with our tags filled, made one last effort to talk Frank into hunting the bare, wind-swept Potato Ridge.

"Never give up," Max lectured. "Those big bucks love to travel the ridges. Besides, it's their only chance now to find feed without digging for it."

While Frank hunted, Max and I broke camp; it was noon before we had all our gear stowed in the boats. We were almost ready to push off when Frank came back. He carried the liver and heart of a deer and was as happy as a kid. He grinned while babbling about how he'd waited downwind of a fresh migration trail.

"Man, this buck strolled up prouder'n a rich playboy. He had his nose in the wind and he looked mean in a way, you know? Maybe a cougar had chased him — I saw a whole lot of cat tracks. Anyway, he watched his back trail. Another funny thing, his mouth was open as if he was going to bite someone." (It turned out that at sometime in the past his jawbone had been badly damaged.)

Frank caressed his rifle. "Just one shot! And he's fatter'n a Thanksgiving turkey."

Thus, I saw the old buck again. I helped Frank drag him down to the nearest beach where we picked him up with the boats.

Seeing our eight deer in a row I began to feel a bit hoggish. Our guilty feelings were soon alleviated by the arrival of a native family. They never spoke, just stood by the truck staring at all the fine meat. Without speaking we rearranged the load so that a fine fat doe was left over and we presented this as a gift to the family.

Frank remained very quiet on the way

home. When Max noticed it he asked if Frank still thought that Tatlayoko was too far to go, or involved taking too much gear.

"No," came the reply. "Everything was just about perfect. I guess it's a lot easier being 'lucky' when you go to the right place. And taking all the comforts of home doesn't hurt either.

By the way, what's your recipe for goulash?"

Of course, Max wouldn't neglect an important item like that, and in the end both Frank and I received a handwritten copy of his specialty. I think it might interest you; it reads like this:

Max Winkler's Goulash Recipe

Take two pounds or more of good quality venison (such as ours) and cut it into bite-size chunks. Fry it in an open pan until it's deliciously brown. Then take a pound, or more of onions, a little garlic, and dice all into small cubes; fry also until brown. Next, mix venison and onions together in a pressure cooker or other covered pot; add salt and pepper to taste; add a few caraway seeds and a couple of small red paprika shoots. Let it all simmer until the meat is done. If you add a little water from time to time you'll get a wonderful gravy.

Good luck and good cooking.~Max

P.S. Don't forget the paprika or the whole delicious mess is just another stew.

***

Stew or goulash, whatever you want to call it, I've tasted it and Max was right. It's a delicious mess. But be it goulash or a hunting trip, if you follow Maximilian's recipe, you just can't go wrong.

1969

It was with serious reservations that I wrote this story in 1969. The late Ed. G. Meade, who once edited the pages of the Northwest Sportsman and was then the Secretary Manager of the B.C. Wildlife Federation, encouraged me to write this expose about those so-called sportsmen who hunted along the Alaska Highway during the late season.

When I completed the assignment Ed shook his head. He had not counted on so much "honesty." He urged me to use pseudonyms because he felt I might suffer harm from certain sides. The story did create a bit of a stir too, the Vancouver Sun commented on it and so did BC Outdoors Magazine.

Chapter 7:

The Poachers

Verne Plager had been silent for the better part of that cold November morning. Like me he was looking for caribou or moose that might cross the road ahead of us. While I was busy steering my four-by-four pick-up, Verne was busy directing the warm air flow of the truck's heater to thaw either our cold feet or the iced-up windows. Suddenly he spoke. "Man, look at that country, what a moose pasture!"

The truck skidded and bounced over the rough, snow-covered trail that had branched away from the Alaska High way and probably led to a distant oil pipeline or capped gas well. The truck lurched sideways and swayed precariously at the edge of a steep side hill. We had just slithered into a pair of deep ruts that carved up the bad trail.

"No need to watch the trail anymore," I joked, "We are now on a guided tour. Maybe these ruts will take us right to the moose."

"You think so?" Verne asked.

"Sure, unless all the moose are hiding today."

"Yeah," Verne replied, "like all the moose along all the other exploration roads we've tried. I used to know a time, back home in the Cariboo, when I could've bet my last bullet that we'd find at least fresh tracks; and in less time than we've taken so far. Maybe this country is all shot up or shot out."

Fighting the jerking steering wheel to keep the truck from rattling around in those oversized ruts, I still hadn't seen the moose pasture he'd mentioned. Then we slithered around a sharp curve and a seemingly endless meadow lay directly before us.

"Whoa! I see one." Verne yelled. "Hold it, will you!"

Even before I could safely stop he had bailed out to load his rifle. He pointed it downhill towards a large black form that slowly moved through a patch of burned-over timber.

"It's a bull," he whispered. "Hasn't seen us yet." Then, to my surprise, Verne lowered his rifle again.

"What's wrong?"

"You know darn well what's wrong," he answered. "He's too far away, 200 yards at least and that slope's too steep. I don't feel like dragging any moose carcass all the way uphill. But if you want him, go ahead and shoot."

Meanwhile I had my rifle ready and squinted through the telescope. The bull was large but no great trophy. But then I hadn't driven 1,000 miles from my home in Port Coquitlam this late in the season to hunt record heads: I wanted some prime game meat and the bull I saw would supply that. I fired and the bull dropped instantly.

"How now?" asked Verne, a frown on his face. "Don't you think we should've driven a little further and maybe found a moose a little closer to the truck? Remember what all the local hunters told us? You're not supposed to shoot any game way off in the bush unless you're starving, or crazy, or have a snowmobile to drag it out with."

I didn't blame Verne for questioning my wisdom; he didn't know that I carried enough nylon rope in the truck to reach the bull. Even without a winch I could haul the meat right up to the road.

It wasn't hard work to retrieve the moose, but the arctic cold certainly bothered us. Although we worked fast to dress and quarter the carcass our feet soon numbed and our knives often stuck fast to our blood-wet fingers. Our breath froze on our clothing and when a cloud of grey mist drifted in from the west it coated the whole scene, us included, with glistening hoar-frost.

"One more moose to go," Verne said through his ice-coated balaclava as he closed the tailgate. "Now let's get the hell out of here and find a friendly motel. I'd hate to camp out again." We had slept the previous night near the Bucking Horse River in the truck under the low canopy. For heat we had kept our gasoline lantern burning; it hadn't been too uncomfortable at first but in the morning my thermometer showed a brittle -5°F - inside the camper. Getting up was disgustingly uncomfortable.

"Let's go to Mason Creek Lodge," Verne suggested. "That's the place we passed this morning, where all the moose and caribou dangled from the meat poles."

We were lucky at the lodge, the hunter's cabin - that's what they called it- was still vacant. Jerry Aven, the friendly proprietor of the lodge, told us that hunting had been good in his neighbourhood.

"You shouldn't have any problems finding another moose," he said. "And with a bit of luck you might even find a herd of caribou. Stay as long as you like. Mind you, if more hunters show up you'll have to move over some and share the facilities." Verne had already spotted the cabin's oil heater and that prompted his quick agreement.

During the evening four other hunters moved in with us.

They had hunted with snowmobiles during the day and all of them looked half-frozen.

For the next three days Verne and I hunted

along the many miles of exploration roads that criss-crossed the country from one horizon to the other, but without success. We saw three great timber wolves and a flock of sharp-tailed grouse, that's all. But the evenings at the cabin with hunters for roommates were most interesting; fascinating, in fact.

During our stay we shared the cabin with nearly a dozen hunters and listened to some amazing hunting yarns. Most of them were local people, from Fort St. John or Dawson Creek, and they used snowmobiles to great advantage. Some of these men claimed, and rather proudly, that it is a cinch to hunt caribou and moose from these machines.

One of our acquaintances, a man from Dawson Creek, had killed a moose and two caribou that first day of our stay and offered to rent us his machine.

"Got to lay low for a day," he said, "at least 'til my oldest son comes up from home to take 'em off my hands and bring some more tags. But I ain't finished huntin' yet."

When I questioned the legitimacy of his operation he answered that he could kill six of each, caribou and moose. "I got four more kids, so all I got to do is buy more licences and tags." With a sly grin he continued. "If I'm lucky I can still sell some of the horns to the odd Yankee sportsman that passes through skunked. They pay about $50 for a good set. I suppose the poor beggars go home and brag about their marksmanship," he chuckled.

Another hunter from the same area said that he'd shot 14 caribou in one day once. He didn't tell exactly when or where and I couldn't check out his statements but this, in essence, is what he told us.

"I had three partners with me when we found this whole herd of stupid caribou, about 60 of 'em. We rounded 'em up like so many cattle; it was in a frozen swamp, you know. I hid myself at the edge of some scrub timber and the others chased the dumb beasts in circles. Every time they came by I cut loose. I uncorked every damn round in my gun and then some; a whole box. When it was all over we had 14. We smuggled 'em all home too. It was easy." It might have been easy but I wondered if it was such a good idea.

One morning Verne and I passed a parked truck on the 186 Mile Road and saw moose tracks. Obviously the moose had crossed over to our right and into a thick section of bush. We stopped to investigate and heard a strange sound on our left.

Verne grabbed his rifle. It was really cold then, -30°F. When I stepped from the warm cab I froze before I could even shiver. Then the strange sound came again; it was like the cry of a child. Verne looked at me and shrugged. Then another sound drifted through the bush; this time we heard it more clearly. I could've sworn that it was the bray of a mule. Then a movement among the spindly trees caught my attention - a black form had brushed snow off a tree. Verne trained his binoculars in that direction. Another bray, closer now, drifted across —but this time Verne collapsed in hysterical laughter. After he'd wiped a tear from his eye he spoke.

"You know what that is? It's a hunter! Imagine!"

The form had come closer still and presently I identified the human shape. He wore a dark green overcoat and a black fur cap. As he approached he slipped and fell over a hidden log, scrambled to his feet again and, although he now saw our truck, he continued to "hee" and "haw" as if he were being paid for it.

"Is he trying to scare the moose out of that bush?" I asked.

Verne didn't answer at first. Finally after the man had crossed the road and disappeared into the bush on the other side, Verne spoke. "You know, I've heard about jackass hunters before, but never seen one at close range."

When we drove on Verne celebrated this "sighting" by reciting a somewhat scandalous version of Robert Service's "Cremation of Sam McGee."

As usual, some new hunters arrived at the lodge that evening. They had the still-steaming carcass of a moose on their truck.

"Got him a couple of hours ago," one of them explained. "I was waiting for my buddy when this young bull walked right up to me."

"I got one too," the other remarked. "He's still in the bush, though, way out in the Rockies to the west - a dandy bull. I lost my spare gas can off the snowmobile; had to leave the machine behind and walked six miles to get out. We're not even sure we can drive the truck all the way in to pick it up.

Say, you fellows have a four-wheel-drive, how about coming in with us? It's good moose country, better than average, and there's some caribou too. You'll get your game for sure and in case we get stuck you could help us out. That trail's no real trouble for a four-by-four."

"We can try it," I answered, and Verne replied that he'd love to see the Rocky Mountains.

It snowed hard the following night. The temperature had risen to -15°F but at 6 a.m. it dropped right down again and a thick freezing fog hid the scenery.

We drove very carefully on this strange trail, the truck felt awfully stiff while skidding and plowing through some deep ruts and old washouts. Only one lonely taillight of the other truck showed us the way. It was nearly 9 a.m. before the first light of a grey dawn crept into the frozen world.

Suddenly, the lead truck stopped. I climbed out and walked over to see if our new hunting acquaintances needed help. A flash of flame burst from the driver's window, almost singeing my face, and the sharp muzzle blast deafened me. I jumped back and then saw the reason for the shooting. A herd of moose stood in some brush to the left of the road. There was more firing. The animals milled about a great bull whose antlers seemed as large as tabletops, and then they ran off.

The other hunters must've fired a dozen shots before a slim cow moose finally dropped and lay still. Without even stopping to investigate their kill they drove ahead to hunt more moose. Two miles up the trail we caught up with them. They told us that their snowmobile and the moose carcass from the previous day were nearby and that they intended to pick them up before they returned to the bull and cow.

"How many moose are you going to kill?" I asked. "As many as we can get," came the reply.

Thoroughly disgusted with this, Verne urged me to drive on and leave them to their own devices.

"I don't want to be part of their operation," he said. "And I hope they get stuck in here so they'll have to stay and eat the meat. It would serve them right, you know." We drove on and pondered what we'd seen.

Verne mused out loud, "It seems to me that our game regulations have too many loopholes. I bet those guys fill the tags for their whole neighbourhood before they go home."

"I guess they feel that the simple possession of a tag entitles them to the game," I said.

"Yeah," Verne replied, "that's about it. I'm not too learned when it comes to all the technical points of the game laws, who is? Still, I always thought that each license holder had to do his own hunting."

"Should we report them to the authorities?" I asked.

"It's not a bad idea," Verne replied. "But do you know what can happen to us? First off, we'll have to prove our complaints beyond a shadow of a doubt or there'll be a case against us for 'malicious prosecution' or some such thing.

"Then, even if we could drag them before a court we might spend half the winter in this neighbourhood without pay. All they'd need is a good lawyer to get the case delayed a half-dozen times and we'd both be broke before spring. And we can hardly overlook the fact that today we might need their help to get back out of this country."

I had looked at the odometer and quickly calculated that we were at least 30 miles off the Alaska Highway; if we got stuck -or the truck broke down- Verne was right, we'd be only too happy to beg for their assistance

Suddenly, the fog lifted and we found ourselves among the eroded domes and lazy ridges of the Rockies. The sun glared.

A crooked little river, ice-bound now, meandered through the wide valley on our left and moose as well as caribou sign was abundant. At noon we stopped to eat our lunch and at 1 p.m. we turned back. Verne had an idea.

"Let's drive past the other fellows this time and let them follow us, otherwise they might shoot more moose yet."

It was sound advice. The boys had loaded

all their meat and wrestled the snowmobile onto their overloaded truck when we passed. Fifteen minutes later, as I rounded a tricky curve and happened to glance in the rear-view mirror, I saw the blurry image of a moose crossing the road behind us. I completed the turn and stopped.

It was a large cow, in no hurry to get away; she just wandered through a thick patch of brush and stopped 200 yards away to look us over.

"I don't want a cow," Verne said, "But let's wait and see what these other guys will do."

The big animal still eyed us somewhat suspiciously; occasionally she nipped a tender shoot off a bush.

Then the other truck came along. Verne reached for his rifle, jumped from the cab and loaded it. He was suddenly in a hurry.

The other hunters had seen the cow too. A rifle barrel poked from their cab window— just as Verne fired and the cow dropped dead.

The other hunters pulled the rifle back and drove up to us. They were quite indignant about Verne's shooting.

"I was all set to pull the trigger," one of them said, "and you blast it right out from under my nose."

I had to laugh. I had never seen Verne like this. Always easy-going, Verne, was now actually mad.

"You're so right," he snarled. "If that poor old cow had to die anyway, I figured that I was entitled to kill her. I've got a tag too, you know. My own at that."

"Well, if that's the way you feel about it."

"No, damn it! That is not the way I feel," Verne snapped.

"It's what's fair and legal."

The other fellow's face looked puzzled for a moment, and then he turned, climbed back into his truck and drove off. It was the last we saw of him. Later we learned that he and his partner had indeed killed another moose that day.

The moon had risen high before we finished the big job of dressing and loading the meat. Verne smiled. His nose was dead white from the frost and his hands and feet were stiff with cold, but he smiled. Back in the truck and heading for ' home he spoke- only then did I realize that he'd remained silent throughout the butchering job.

"You know," he said, "this is beautiful game country — much finer than the Cariboo." He paused for a moment.

"That reminds me— we haven't seen hide or hair of the reindeer yet. Woodland Caribou— that's what Jerry Aven called them. You still want to go after 'em?"

"Not really," I answered. "We can always come back next year."

"I'm not so sure about that," Verne mused. "The way these guys are hunting up here there may be none left. By the way, you'd better drive carefully from now on- next year too- I don't think those guys would give us a tow now."

I agreed with him.

1970

For many reasons my good friend Pat Wright, of Princeton, B.C., (who guides sportsmen in the Ashnola region) had told me about "his" sheep. Finally (although I had acquired an aversion to climbing tall mountains) I decided to hike into this wondrous region of tall timber, open slopes and bunch grass to see it for myself. Eventually I spent four seasons on horseback in this province's most game-rich real estate. This is the story of my first honest try to bag a California bighorn ram.

Chapter 8:

Ashnola Sheep Hunt

"Look! Sheep!" Dan Bowers called excitedly. I nearly spilled my supper into our tiny campfire as I craned my neck to follow his pointing finger.

"That dry ravine over on the left and near the bottom of that grey triangular cliff. Just look up and along the trail- where the cows are. See 'em now?"

Three dark shadows moved along the open

side hill; slowly it seemed, taking a bite here and there. They showed no sign of fear or alarm, no concern for us or the hundred-odd Hereford cattle that grazed directly below them. I hung my soup pot on the ridge pole of our lean-to and reached for the binoculars.

Even with the binoculars it was impossible to see the size and shape of the sheep's' horns. And the fading light didn't help any either, as the September sun disappeared behind the massive ridges of the Okanagan Range.

One animal turned and its white rump patch flashed. Dan, watching through his telescope, commented: "Man, did you ever see anything like that before? The rear end of that sheep looks like a pair of white pants hiking along the hill. Come on, let's get 'em if we can."

Dan raced for the cover of a dry wash-out while I got my carbine from the lean-to. Fifteen minutes later we peeked out from behind a large boulder, panting like marathon runners at the finish line.

"No more cover from here on, "Dan gasped."What now?" We had just learned our first lesson in stalking the beautiful and all-too-rare California bighorn sheep. Earlier we'd discovered that there is no need to go to California in search of this cousin to the Rocky

Mountain bighorn. The B.C. Fish and Game Branch had told us that small bands of California bighorns range all the way north - from California, through eastern Oregon, Idaho and Washington-into B.C. Almost all of these sheep are protected by closed seasons.

Until 1954 most bands of bighorns were found in B.C., but a good number of them have since been trapped and transferred to the western United States. In British Columbia, now, California bighorns range from the U.S. border in the south Okanagan to the Bella Coola road on the Chilcotin plateau. The latest estimate indicates that between 1,200 and 1,500 of these sheep graze in B.C. - about four-fifths of the world's present California bighorn population.

For a number of years I had known about many of B.C.'s better sheep ranges. But every opening day, sometime between the first and last day of September, depending on the game management area, I was either too busy building boats in Vancouver or else too lazy to go hunting. I had looked at many steep slopes in the Shulaps Range. I had hunted the nearly 10,000-foot-high Yalakom Mountains. And once I'd crawled about the shale-covered domes of mountains in the Taseko Lakes region.

After these short but hard lessons in lung and leg exercises, I had decided that sheep should die peacefully. I changed my mind about this when one of my far and high-ranging hunting friends told me that the Ashnola Mountains near the fruit-growing center of Keremeos would be easy to climb.

He'd been there in previous seasons and had actually seen the Californians, but had never bagged a ram. Once, he told me, a bunch of legal-size rams had nearly run him down. At that time he had fired his rifle (I was too polite to quiz him about his abilities as a marksman). In any event, after listening to these tales I warmed to the idea of sheep hunting.

Next I met Dan Bowers and he encouraged me further."Never mind the steep mountains. Let's just go there and give this sheep hunting a try."

Before our trip we gathered every bit of sheep hunting information we could find. Dan, who is a native of Toronto, confessed that he had always dreamed of hunting in the west and had long been searching the library shelves for information and advice.

Then I made a pre-season visit to the Ashnola Mountains. Pat Wright, who is an old friend and a guide in the area, invited me to ride up with him and take a few pictures. On that trip during the last week in May we counted over 150 sheep, among them 24 fair sized rams. Big mule deer also roamed the range and one evening we saw over 100.

When opening day came Dan and I were ready. I had weighed my pack and was amazed to learn that food, a cook pot and a sleeping bag, can add up to 50 pounds. I hated to think what including my camera, rifle, cigarettes and the odd candy bar would do to the weight. On a cloudy day we drove to the Ashnola campsite where a conservation officer had set up a check station. We learned that 17 rams had already been bagged.

We left the car behind and after three long breath-robbing miles we crossed Ewart Creek and faced the steep mountains. We crossed Juniper Creek shortly after and the clouds began to lift. Sweating and gasping, we clawed and climbed on through the last steam bath cloud, over a last ridge and through the last timber. Ahead lay a steep, wide-open and lazily rounded slope. To our astonishment, we saw herds of cattle.

Dan had focused his binoculars and now groaned in disappointment. "What kind of sheep did you have in mind?" he asked. "This place looks like a barnyard. We should've brought a pair of clippers to give the sheep a shearing. I've never heard or read about hunting sheep in among a bunch of cows. I thought wild sheep were supposed to live way up in the rocks and shale. Suppose these Californians haven't read the same book?"

He pointed towards a snow-covered ridge about 10 miles distant. "That looks more like the territory we want, but I'll be darned if I can carry my junk that far."

On a tiny plateau Dan built a small cooking fire and pre pared lunch. Later, over a cup of coffee, he remarked that the Ashnola is altogether different from the popular image of a mountain sheep's home.

Dan's observations were interrupted by the arrival of a pack-train. Rocks and stones clattered as the horses scram bled from a nearby ravine. It was Pat's outfit heading down hill with a beautiful three-quarter-curl ram decorating one of the pack animals.

Pat stopped to adjust saddle and pack cinches, and while he busied himself with the ropes and gear he gave us some pointers on sheep hunting, Ashnola style. "Never mind the cows," he drawled. "The sheep graze right among 'em. Don't shoot 'em though," he grinned. "The cows I mean."

"So it's Sheep Country after all," Dan said, his face brightening. Quickly he doused the campfire and we went hunting. The hills proved as dry and burnt as yesterday's toast.

Bunchgrass, belly-high to a steer, covered almost the entire small, level plateau. Pasture sage bloomed and many different grasses blended to create a greyish- green background for protruding rocks and weathered cliffs.

Wash-outs had carved almost straight cuts and furrows down into Juniper Creek; the pushed-up edges were covered with alder bush, jack pine and golden aspen. These overgrown furrows provided escape lanes for the sheep.

We spent most of our first afternoon hiking and climbing, surveying the hills with binoculars at short intervals, but not finding the sheep. Then, as the sun threatened to drop behind the snowy ridge of the Cathedral Mountains and we were back at camp getting supper, Dan had spotted the sheep. Our first mad dash began.

The boulder was indeed the last bit of cover for us. Carefully I pushed my binoculars into position. The sheep hadn't gone away, but they were facing us.

"Just like it says in the books," Dan whispered. "They've seen us already."

The range was still about 500 yards and in the fast-fading light we could only watch the animals - two ewes and a lamb. They looked like deer, a little smaller perhaps, but nearly the same color, and every inch as graceful. Their short curved horns reminded me of domestic goat horns, nine to ten inches long and flattened towards the tips. After a while the sheep lay down; they were still watching us but they weren't frightened.

Ice had formed on my soup when we returned to camp. In our excitement we hadn't noticed the cold wind and for the first time I was happy to have packed a good, heavy, sleeping robe.

Next morning I was awakened by loud swearing. A cowboy had ridden up the trail and his horse had shied when it saw our lean-to. As I looked out the pony nearly threw its rider.

Later that day we met the same cowboy again, and he helped us pack a mule deer buck to our camp. He told us that he'd punched cows throughout the Ashnola range and knew the area and its sheep well. He said he'd shot a ram once with horns that measured nearly 36 inches around the curl and almost 16 inches around the base.

California bighorns, like other wild sheep, mature at approximately three-and-a-half years of age, but their horns grow until they die. Normally this happens in their tenth to thirteenth year.

That night it froze again. The sun rose as we reached a nameless peak the cowboy had said was a good place to spot sheep. The high ranges all around sparkled. Frozen dew drop lets glinted like diamonds in the grass and a trace of stubborn snow clung to the shadow side of the fallen logs in the burns. Huge blue grouse thundered off our trail, and now and again a calf bawled for its mother in some hidden ravine. Fat Herefords grazed in scattered bands all over the hill right up to the snow line.

By noon we had searched two basins without seeing any sheep. We had just settled down to eat lunch when Dan pointed to a steep ridge beyond the third basin, "There's our cowboy friend again." Dan suddenly became excited. "Look! Up where the cowboy hit the timber. Three animals are coming down. Look at 'em go!"

For the sheep hunter there is no sight as thrilling as three big rams coming straight towards him. A massively built ram led the way through shale slides, over windblown logs in the burn, across the creek bottom and on to our side. He stopped, his companions caught up to him, and the three sheep came on together.

"Keep a-coming," Dan prayed aloud.

Suddenly the rams froze in their tracks. They were still 500 yards away and looking straight at us. In our fascination we hadn't moved and were in a hopeless position, out in the open with only bunchgrass for cover.

The lead ram was nearly black in color and sported almost fully curled horns. The other rams were more of a reddish brown, but they too, without doubt, had legal-size horns. They were all nervous - their stubby little ears twitched and once the two younger rams looked back. With the old ram standing at attention and staring our way, we were forced to make the next move.

I put my hat on top of a stick and we crawled away to a row of fir trees. When I dared to take my first look from the good cover I was sure we had our ram in the bag. All three animals kept staring at my battered old Stetson. We travelled downhill towards them, going from tree to tree as fast as possible. A hundred yards closer.... two hundred yards.

"Close enough?" Dan asked. I nodded.

Ever so slowly we raised our guns over a fallen log.

"Where are they?" I asked.

The rams were running bouncing away from us to vanish among the willows at the creek bottom.

The whole stalking episode had taken about ten minutes.

Shortly, we saw two other hunters hike along the creek and cross where the rams had disappeared; we hoped they would chase our trophies back to us, but no ram showed up again. We waited for an hour and used our binoculars to check every stump and rock- and saw nothing.

Dan was the first to recover his wits along with his sense of humour.

"Good thinking old man," he said grinning. "I suppose you remembered just in time that Pat Wright has already gone home for the season? Without his pack-train how could we get two big rams out of this place? It's about twelve miles to the car isn't it?"

"You still like sheep hunting?" I asked.

1971

I suppose one may argue where the actual boundary between the East and West Kootenays lies. Some folks define all of B.C. east of Kootenay Lake as the East Kootenays, but I was not so choosey when Mr. Jim Railton, former publisher and owner of the Northwest Sportsman magazine asked me to go east and bring back a deer hunting story for his readers. It was a very good experience for me to see new territory and I enjoyed the whole trip immensely. I trust you will too.

Chapter 9:

West Kootenay Safari: The Author's Jackpot

"Are you absolutely certain this is good deer hunting country?" My friend and partner Frank Kasa expressed his doubts for the umpteenth time.

We were driving the road that winds north from Creston, B.C. along the picturesque shores of Kootenay Lake, searching for the creek and valley Ed Meade had marked on a map for us.

Low November clouds hid most of the mountainous scenery now and the waters of the great lake lay calm and depressingly grey below us.

"Sure," I replied. "Ed manages the government information centre and he got his information from a game biologist in Cranbrook. We can't miss," I joked. "Besides, what ever happened to your spirit of adventure? Don't you like seeing new country?"

Frank just mumbled something about our good old hunting ground near Princeton and the Bridge River Valley, where in previous seasons we had managed to satisfy our annual craving for venison.

"Never mind all that," I interrupted. "When I've travelled this country before, in good weather, I've always seen whitetail deer but never had the time to hunt. There are herds of elk in these hills too. And the season in this game management area is about the most liberal in the province. If you have a tag you can even shoot a cow elk."

Ignoring my last remark, Frank asked, "What's the name of this creek again - where our turn-off is?"

"Akokli," I replied, wondering if I had

pronounced it properly.

"Funny name," he mused. "I wonder what it means."

Frank, who was born and raised in Vienna, Austria, had a hard time wrapping his tongue around the name. "I hope it means plenty of game, huh?"

At a grocery store in Boswell we asked directions, since few of the creek bridges displayed name signs. As it was, we had already driven too far north. Our road turned out to be very steep and muddy. I had to stop and engage the truck's four-wheel-drive mechanism to climb the grade. Two thousand feet above the level of the lake we finally skidded to a halt in a wash-out where the ground was as soft and slippery as soap.

"This has got to be it, my boy," I said. And then I backed 50 yards downhill to a fairly level spot and parked. We were right in the clouds now - a thin white mist that opened up occasionally to allow us a glimpse at the lake below. Frank still wasn't convinced that we were in good game habitat.

We looked around at a thick growth of pine, interlaced with shedding tamarack, spruce, cedar, aspen and birch. Patches of old crusty snow from an early storm and a lot of underbrush would make for noisy, difficult walking. Frank did not believe we were in the West Kootenay game paradise he had heard about.

Suddenly he snapped alert. "Hey! Look here! There are some mighty big deer in this neighbourhood." He pointed to a set of fresh footprints that were at least four inches long. "And here too. They're fresh. See this." He bent down to show me that water was still seeping into the tracks. "Must be elk, eh?"

Fog, brush and snow could not hold him back now. He disappeared under the canopy of the truck and exactly two minutes later emerged ready to go hunting. And I sure worked up a healthy sweat trying to keep up with him.

Around the first curve we found some bear tracks. The huge imprints looked fresh enough to suggest that we had scared the animal off with our somewhat noisy approach. For the rest of that long day we poked around.

Frank even climbed to the mountain's summit in an attempt to get out of the drifting fog — but we did not see game. I met a couple of local footsloggers like us, likewise unlucky, and a family on a Sunday drive in a chain equipped pick-up truck. Towards evening light rain fell. We camped in the back of my truck under the canopy. At 10 p.m. the drizzle worked itself into a howling rainstorm. Frank voiced his disappointment.

"Here we are, hundreds of miles from our homes on the coast and the weather is no different. Oh, what's the use..." By midnight he drifted off to sleep. The next morning dawned cold and partially clear. The ground was frozen.

"This is worse," Frank complained. "We'll never sneak up on anything now." But then, as if to prove himself wrong, and before I could finish my elaborate breakfast, he went hunting.

I was sorry that Frank had not been able to at least see some game. I poured myself another cup of coffee and drank it slowly before I set out on his trail.

I had hiked about 50 yards along the trail - not being particularly careful or quiet- when I came around a curve and met a buck head on. He was right in the middle of the road, sporting three long, pitchfork prongs on each antler, looking like a prince. He flicked his tail and his eats twitched forward when he recognized the danger. With the blast of my shot he dropped -a prime mule deer - just what I wanted for my freezer.

When Frank returned at noon I had the buck all dressed and hanging to cool, from a makeshift tripod. Frank had still not seen any game, but he was happy for me and soon began to kid me about my good fortune. Trying to sound sour, he said that I was just plain lucky all of the time.

"Listen, now that you've got yours, can't we go somewhere else?" Frank asked.

"Sure, we can drive to LaFrance creek. Ed marked that on our map as well. I don't know what that country looks like, but if you think it'll make the difference we can go. Let's have lunch and then pack."

By late afternoon we found the new area; it was only eight miles further north. The road there was not nearly as steep but strangely enough was covered in deep snow. Again we found plenty of frozen deer and elk tracks. But here, unlike our last spot, the mountainside above the road was fairly open. The forest consisted mainly of tamarack, broken up by the stands of aspen and birch; and we could see lots of ground in among the trees.

The mountain rose steeply, and showed broken cliffs, many with 45 degree slopes. Frank looked the terrain over carefully before announcing that it would be sheer murder to climb around in all that rockery, especially in the frozen snow.

"Just hunt along the road then," I told him. "If you see a buck uphill — shoot. It won't be much of a chore to skid him down. By the way, doe season's open here too."

"Don't want any of them," Frank replied. "Bucks taste just as good and I want a trophy."

"Fussy, aren't you? What tags have you got?"

"The whole lot," he grumbled. And then quickly he added that he wasn't really greedy or trigger happy, but that he had heard the government supposedly manages our game with the revenue from game tags.

He figured that he should support good management by buying lots of tags. "Cost me a small fortune too. Right now it seems it's going to be a lean winter for me and the wife has made a case against anymore hunts. You know, she told me that I had better bring some good meat home this time or she'll spend our money on beef instead of game tags and hunting trips."

He laughed. "Some logic, eh? As if beef could take the place of good venison." For the last hour of daylight we cruised the road trying to find a good game crossing before it was time for supper and a night's rest. A hint of snow was in the air.

At dawn next day the sky was still grey, but no new snow had fallen. Frank said, "After breakfast I am going up that road as far as I can. Where are you headed?"

I had noticed a logging road the night before and thought that since we were parked close by I would hike up the mountain to find another buck. "Got a hungry family to feed, you know."

"Good luck," he said, and really meant it.

Of course Frank chose to walk the road for obvious reasons: at over 50 years of age he would have to be crazy to make a steep climb and invite a heart attack. The higher I climbed the greater my respect for Frank's wisdom grew. I had never been on a road so steep before. Wet with perspiration, I reached its end two hours later.

There seemed to be a basin or hanging valley further up, just the kind of place deer and elk would use as a last resort before the next snowstorm drove them down for the duration of winter. A narrow game trail led towards it and plenty of fresh signs showed that it was indeed well travelled.

I sat down for a rest. The sky was still grey.

But now the clouds had lifted completely clear of the valley. Swarms of tiny birds buzzed the tamarack, pecking seeds from the small pods on the naked branches. The snow and the ground below were carpeted with brown, shed tamarack needles. The frost had made a crunchy carpet of this. I ate a chocolate bar and later lit my pipe, watching its smoke drift slowly downhill. I noticed that the wind was in my favour.

My pipe was cold when I happened to glance downhill. Fifteen feet away grew a skinny willow bush at the edge of the road. I looked, then blinked my eyes and stared in disbelief at the twin brother of my buck from the day before who stood motionless behind that flimsy willow screen and stared right back at me.

My rifle was out of easy reach, leaning against a stump behind me. I reached for it, wondering how long that buck had been watching me. I had not heard him come.

The buck saw my movement. He threw up his head and bounced into thick cover above the road.

Later, when I told Frank about it he laughed. "Didn't hear him coming, huh? I know, you're stone deaf. Don't listen to me either, do you? Never seen the ghost of a buck myself."

While we discussed the day's futile hunting efforts the first flakes of snow drifted from the sky. By 3 p.m. it was too dark to hunt. Frank seemed to be cheered by this and by my missing a second buck. He made us a hot lunch, tea, and even supper, all the while smiling and expressing hopes that tomorrow he would get his trophy.

"If the snow keeps falling all night long I'll be able to catch one right on the road. Maybe we'll have to camp here until spring," he added thoughtfully.

In spite of my warm bedding, I lay awake most of the night. Frank, too, tossed and turned enough to make the truck's springs squeal like a herd of pigs. By morning only four inches of snow had fallen; it was not nearly enough to force the game down.

"Now you won't even be able to climb up that skid road again," he grumbled. "What's the matter with this crazy weather? Another three weeks and it'll be Christmas. A green Christmas, I suppose."

"A quarter-mile from here I saw a park-like plateau," I told him. "Let's hunt through it."

"No. You go ahead. I'll keep to the road. But

if we don't get any results we had better get out of here. Try another area on our way home."

"Fair enough."

Fifty yards into the parkland I found my first fresh track leading towards and along another skid road. It was difficult to climb in that new snow; I didn't think I would catch up with the deer, but was determined to climb as high as possible. I slipped often and every 10 steps had to stop and rest. Thus, I had travelled about a mile from the truck and a good 1,000 feet above it, when I saw game — and everything happened rather quickly after that.

Stopping just below the crest of an extremely steep grade I looked through a thin bush — a pair of mule deer ears moved about. Then the head of a doe came into view. I raised my rifle carefully and peered through its scope. I was trying to make up my mind whether to take her when antler tips suddenly showed behind her.

Both deer came down the road directly towards me, only the naked bush between us. I nearly panicked and shot the doe, thinking that she would surely see me first and lead her boyfriend to safety. But at 20 yards distance the buck showed clearly alongside the doe, and I fired.

The doe must have been pleasantly preoccupied to come this close, but before I recovered from the shot's recoil she had vanished into a thicket. The buck made a tremendous leap forward. He was almost on top of me before he saw me. He put on the brakes, digging his heels into the snow. Then he reared up and skidded towards me on his hind legs. In that moment I saw that my first bullet had only creased his massive neck. I suppose he knew that he was trapped.

There was only one way out for him - right into me or over me. I am still amazed at how many details I saw in that split second: his fully developed four-point antlers; his thick and ruffled winter coat; his blind right eye. Then, thinking that he might deliberately charge into me, I fired from the hip. The heavy bullet knocked him down. He dropped to his belly and slid right into me, one of his antlers knocking against my legs. Thirty yards downhill we both stopped; the buck hung up on bush and I was hung up on his antlers.

I wasn't hurt in the slide, just covered with snow. It was easy to slide the buck to the truck and a waiting, luckless Frank.

Frank refused to take a turn at the wheel on the trip home and driving was a tiring business. "You had all the fun," he said, grinning. "Now you might as well do some work. I'll watch out the window and look for another buck."

Near Christina Lake he spotted a fat whitetail buck- and missed him. "Darn it. I had him in my sights, but good. Then just as I started to squeeze the trigger I saw his flag come up. He must've out-jumped that bullet."

I did a bit of friendly ribbing and said that his bullet should've been at least three-quarters on its way before the buck's tail came up.

"I guess so," admitted Frank.

I kidded him some more about his slow and selective kind of shooting, realizing all the time that he is the safest and best deer hunting partner I have ever had.

"Hey, listen Frank, want to stay and try for another?" "No. I've had enough for this season. Let the wife eat beef steak until next year."

1974

Since 1968, Atlin has been a magical name and place for me. Some good friends of mine had been there the previous year, brought back some great game and raved about the old mining town and its beautiful surroundings. I just had to go there and experience it for myself.

It was not always easy to find good partners for the 4,000 odd mile round-trip. It was always comparatively expensive to travel that far afield and in these past few years the costs have become almost prohibitive. But one must be exceptionally well equipped for any kind of hunt in far northern regions. The country can be unforgiving.

Atlin was probably our best mountain caribou area; had a good sheep population and the size of its moose is legendary indeed. Grizzlies are still plentiful and on more than one occasion have investigated me thoroughly. In summation, the Atlin wilderness is no place for the inexperienced hunter, but for those who have learned to live and survive in remote wilderness, it is a paradise of immense proportions.

Chapter 10:

Moose Hunt at Fish Lake

Frank Apel paddled his freight canoe silently over the reflection of a fiery sunrise. "See any moose yet?" he asked in a muffled voice.

"Not yet," I replied as quietly, and added that we had probably spooked our girlfriend from the previous evening clean out of the country.

We had seen the old rutting cow moose when returning to camp from the evening hunt. She had watched us paddle past and then broken out of the shoreline bushes into the shallow channel. Stopping about 60 steps short of us the old cow had just stared at the red canoe. Our outboard motor was tilted up at the time and we paddled so that we could, if the occasion arose, legally shoot from the boat.

But we only stopped to view the nosey moose, since cow season wasn't open. Acting on impulse, I had formed my hands into a funnel around my mouth and grunted in imitation of bull moose's love song.

Frank cursed. "Are you crazy?"

It was too late for curses. The old cow had come towards us like a can-can dancer. Since the water was only up to her knees she came fast.

"You stupid son of a ..." was all I heard from Frank's next curse, then he had the motor down, started and we roared away from the cow. Sitting in the bow of the canoe, I had been able to observe the cow's face. The friendly lover's smile seemed to slide right off her long nose until she had the sad look of a basset hound. Finally the water had become too deep for further advances. With her butter-barrel belly hanging in the water, she stopped and stared forlornly at the departing canoe.

At a safe distance Frank had stopped.

"Why in hell did you do that?" he asked. "She almost climbed right in with us and we couldn't even have shot her!"

"It seemed like a good idea at the time," I said, "Think of it as an experiment done in the interests of science. You know, to find out what makes moose tick. How was I to know she'd fall in love with us so quickly?" Frank had laughed then. "True, but I certainly wouldn't appreciated being kissed by her."

The cow still stood in the lake and looked at us. It was too dark to photograph her, so I had suggested that we become the pursuers and drive full tilt towards her.

"Why?" asked Frank. "Why not?" I replied. Then added jokingly, "In the interests of science you could at least make the effort? You start the motor, I'll grunt a few more love notes and then we can go full throttle towards her. Just to see what she'll do next."

I had managed only two guttural coughs before the engine roared into life and the canoe sped towards her at 15 knots.

The poor cow had come apart at the seams. It appeared as if she was going in 27 directions at once. A tall geyser of water and mud had erupted where she stood and as the waters calmed again we had seen our girlfriend disappear between the willows of the swamp. I was certain that we had spooked her too badly and said as much to Frank. He was not convinced.

Parallel to shore and about 30 steps from land we slid silently along. We were almost at the spot we'd seen her depart from the previous evening when I detected a movement behind some shoreline willows.

Frank had seen something as well. "Is that the cow again?"

Through my binoculars I saw the outline of a black animal body and behind it - antler tips! "A bull," I whispered, "behind the cow."

Frank's skill with the paddle brought us quietly closer.

Slowly the shoreline vegetation moved like the scenery on a stage and we could see the cow behind. At 50 paces I motioned to Frank to get ready for a shot.

He nodded, but from his signals I knew that he hadn't yet seen the bull — he was hard to detect because he stood exactly behind and in line with the cow. Only the antler tips and an extra leg betrayed his presence. Frank had exchanged his paddle for his rifle while we drifted slowly in the lazy currents of the channel. At 35 paces we drifted past the cow and suddenly I could see the bull.

Splash! A hungry pike broke the glassy lake surface and almost jumped in my face. Startled, I threw myself back. If we had not been using the outrigger on the canoe we would have wound up swimming.

The bull threw up his head. The cow turned around to look at us. Then Frank's rifle flashed. Through the thunder of the shot I saw cut moose hair and bits of hide fly. With a giant leap the fat old cow jumped over her falling mate and disappeared into the bush. We grabbed the paddles to get to shore and begin the real work.

"So you see," explained Frank to our partners back at camp later than night, "that's how it's done." Horst Pothmann and Sandy Lamberton had hunted elsewhere that day, using their trail bikes to drive along a few ancient mining roads. They hadn't seen any game.

I had been in the Atlin area on several occasions and had always seen lots of game. At my urging, Frank, Horst and Sandy had come to the area with me this time. All three were fellow members of the Port Coquitlam and District Hunting and Fishing Club, all were club directors and Frank was president at the time. If I recall correctly, I needed all my powers of persuasion to convince the gentlemen that a three day drive to Atlin would not be without thrills. But it was the prospect of not having to compete with hordes of weekend hunters that finally convinced them to go north.

Because Frank and I had already seen a pike, we took our fishing gear along the morning after shooting the bull. Horst had caught pike when he lived in Manitoba and promised to do the cooking if we could guide him to the fish. Of course we accepted his generous offer and took him along.

Sandy figured the canoe would be too crowded with four hunters – turned fishermen —and said he wanted to hunt caribou that day anyway. I suspect, however, that he did not yet trust the outrigger-equipped canoe and probably figured he would upset the whole thing if fishing was good.

Again we paddled so as to still-hunt from the canoe on our way to the fishing spot. After all, it might be that the widowed cow had already found another mate. We reached the pike hole in the relatively shallow lake, dropped our anchor over the side and fished. We were also in a good position to spot game.

Meanwhile, the pike flashed all around us like miniature torpedoes. Almost every cast produced a fish. The best bait was a large red and white spoon. I had only brought a small spinning rod equipped with an ancient Quick Junior reel that I usually use for trout fishing, so it was quite a thrill when I hooked and landed a 15-pound pike with my fragile equipment. We kept only fish over eight pounds and any that hurt themselves on the hooks. Ten fish a day was the limit for each of us in those days. In two hours we had 28 and were convinced we could fill the canoe.

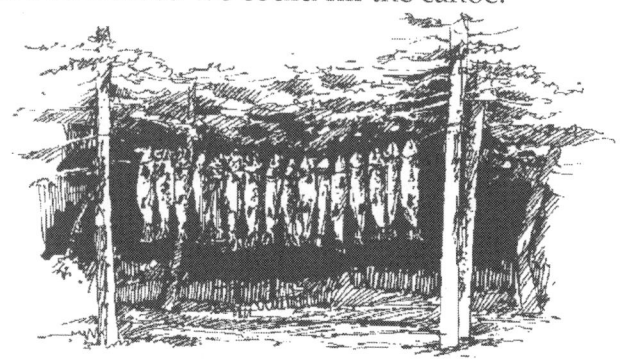

Horst scratched his head as we reminded him of his earlier promise. Sure, I can cook them, but we can't eat them all," he gasped. "What are we going to do? Fine bunch of conservationists you are!"

What he didn't know was that I had brought some pieces of plywood and other items to build a smoke box. The pike would not spoil. We fished until noon and then went back to camp.

Our campsite had been used by generations of local folks and occasional hunters, so it was not surprising to find all the necessary materials to build a very efficient smoker. A piece of stovepipe lay rusting in the bush, along with a roll of chicken wire. We soon had a proper fireplace dug and fortified with rocks and slabs of stone. I nailed the box together, using the chicken wire for a grill and the stovepipe for a vent.

With dry willow wood for fuel, the whole thing was operational in short order. First we cleaned the fish and packed them in pickling salt overnight. The next morning we washed them and hung them on a rope to dry, and then we dunked them in a thick brown sugar solution.

For six hours I sat and tended our smoky fire carefully while the pike were transformed into oversize kippers. Of course Horst had used four pike for supper already. These he had filleted and fried in a beer and flour mixture. They had been delicious, but the pike that were fresh-smoked and still hot tasted even better. The cooled, smoked fish would last until we got home.

Then came an evening I will never forget. We had hunted the lakeshore for a week already and began to believe that our cow moose had left for healthier climates. It was around sunset when we pushed the canoe into some tall reeds and sat still, just listening to the sounds of the surrounding swamp.

For a thousand paces or more we could see the channel. Slowly, night came over the eastern horizon, like a dark blue curtain. The few white cirrus clouds glowed. Then Frank thought he heard the grunting of a bull moose.

"Uggg," came the sound again. There could be no mistake — somewhere in the swamp a moose was calling for a mate.

This time Sandy was with us. We had agreed that he was to get the next shot. Suddenly, from the bench land above our camp came the mournful song of a family of wolves.

"Au-uuuhhh," sounded the chorus, and then somewhat horrid and drawn-out from three other wolf throats "auhuh hhhhhhh." I know wolves and knew that at this time of year they would not be a threat to humans, but I still felt goose bumps rise on my skin.

Frank stood up to look over the bushes and spoke immediately. "A big bull is coming through the swamp to the lakeshore. Hurry, we've got to get to the other side of the channel and into the reeds so we can ambush him."

A dozen hard paddle strokes drove the canoe across the lake and into man-high reeds. Sandy sat up front. I heard the quiet "click" as he put one of his 7mm Remington magnum shells into his rifle's chamber. I had my old 30-

06 with me in case a second rifle should be needed. Since Frank's moose licence was filled he had left his rifle in camp.

Again the "Ugg-uggg" echoed over the lake. We sat motionless. The light evening breeze drifted from the north and travelled the length of the lake. We hoped it would take our scent away from the bull. Suddenly the bull stood like a coal-black monument at the shore and eyed the scenery. He was 200 paces away from us and it didn't seem likely that he would remain there long.

Sandy did not wish to shoot at this range. We had to get closer. Everything depended on Frank now. He pushed the canoe out of the reeds and then kept it very close to the high bank; he bent low to avoid showing the bull a silhouette. Sandy and I lay on the floor of the boat.

The bull moved a little, and then his love notes echoed again across the water. After that he stood with head held high to listen for possible answers.

Shooting light was fading fast now. Besides, we had to keep within the prescribed hunting time limit - from one hour before sunrise until one hour after sunset. We had to hurry now. Eight minutes. Five minutes.

We had come 100 paces closer to the huge bull. Sandy had his rifle resting on the gunwale. He had never killed a big trophy moose before and was excited.

"When?" he asked.

"As long as he's standing still - wait," I counseled. "If he begins to move — fire immediately."

Sandy scrambled to change his glasses. In the excitement he had left his sunglasses on. One minute before closing the bull threw his head up.

"Shoot!!!"

Sandy's bullet flashed out of the barrel. I thought I heard the bullet hit, but the moose was not yet down and gave a startled look in our direction .Sandy called out that he couldn't re-load, his empty cartridge was stuck in the rifle's chamber.

He had used a hand-loaded shell. "You shoot!" he yelled.

"Okay. Stay down!" I was on my feet without realizing it. If the bull was to run I could shoot over top of the reeds. He had to fall now. If he got back into the swamp we could write him off. I knew that. In my scope I saw him lift his right front leg. I fired. The flash of the shot temporarily blinded me. I blinked my eyes a couple of times to refocus, but the bull was suddenly gone.

Then we heard swamp water splash and the death rattle in the hull's throat. Two minutes later everything was over for him. The silence was almost unbearable. Some ducks had flown up after the shots but they were quiet now.

Frank pulled up his hip-waders and stepped over the side. We followed his lead and waded carefully through the reeds and swamp grass. Frank had the battery spotlight at hand. He let its beam play over the scene. With every step we sank knee-deep into the ooze. After 30 paces with our rifles held at the ready, the beam of light illuminated a large dark object on the ground to our left.

"Careful!" he warned. "That could be him."

"This moose is dead," said Sandy as he stepped towards the huge bull. Huge was the only, word to describe what we had killed. The antlers measured' 65 inches across. They were symmetrically formed and a great trophy. Sandy beamed with joy.

"Finally I thought I'd never get a good moose for my collection."

We found two bullet holes. One bullet had driven head-on through the hull's rather large bell into the chest. It hit, alas, a little too high for the hull's heart. The second, mine, had broken the right shoulder joint, just where I had aimed for in order to anchor the beast. Both shots were deadly. Sandy's bullet had torn the hull's jugular vein to shreds.

We field-dressed and quartered the carcass immediately, but the quarters were too heavy for the three of us to bring to the canoe. So we took only the heart and liver with us and returned to camp where Horst had supper ready – smoked pike with potatoes and asparagus.

The next morning all of us set out in both canoes and brought the meat back to camp. Right after that Frank and Sandy went boating again, 30 miles down the big lake to look for caribou. Horst and I remained in the camp, lazing about and smoking more fish.

Two nights later the weather changed.

"Did you say Frank and Sandy were coming back today?" asked Horst.

"No. Tomorrow or Wednesday. And if they don't show up we'll have to look for them on Thursday."

Horst glanced at the boiling lake and the huge white breakers that crashed onto the pebble beach. The wind almost blew the glasses off his nose and his eyes were watering.

"But in this wild weather... I mean, if Frank in his large canoe can't manage, how can we in your smaller canoe?"

"Very carefully," I replied, "with the outrigger and my motor we can do it. Only very slowly. Otherwise we have to drive the truck to Atlin and hire a float plane, eh? But I think those two know enough about canoes and rough water. They know what they can't do. Besides, they have an outrigger too."

That afternoon we took the two trail bikes and made a long reconnaissance trip on a number of old, overgrown mining roads. We found a few abandoned mines but no game. Some times the wind blew so hard it threatened to knock us off the bikes. Shortly before 5 p.m. it began to drizzle.

On the hill above camp I stopped to take a good look at the huge swamp that surrounded the little lake. I spotted two black dots in the channel where I knew no spots ought to be. With my zoom glasses I identified a bull and a cow moose in the shallow water. It seemed they were feeding on the abundant aquatic vegetation.

We headed for camp, where a surprise awaited us. The fire was burning brightly and our two partners sat under a tarp nearby warming themselves. Both laughed at our surprised faces.

"Say, are you guys crazy, canoeing on a day like this?"

"Hell, it wasn't so bad," said Frank. "This morning it was beautiful at the far end, smooth as glass. Until noon we fished at Chehalis Creek." He pointed to a huge char that hung from his truck's roof rack. He's 25 pounds, I bet. It only got rough when we left there. The last seven miles we surfed along as best as we could."

Horst broke into the conversation and reminded me of the moose.

"You see any?" asked Sandy.

"Yup. Bull and a cow. In the channel."

Sandy advised the three of us to go after them. "The lake is alright if you watch out for the breakers. Don't worry, I'll keep an eye out if you get into trouble."

The mile-long drive across the lake to the channel was mighty unpleasant. As on most long, narrow lakes, the waves rolled very close together. The wind had piled them into four-foot-high combers that always threatened to come over the gunwale.

Once Horst called out to me to turn back or steer into the wind. He was afraid of capsizing,

I knew, because he could not swim. To show him how bad it would be to head into the steep waves I turned the canoe a little. He had a lapful of water and he hollered again.

Without my outrigger, which I had especially designed and built for such weather, I would not have risked the trip. With it, I could ride broadside to the waves and get no more than spray or foam in the boat. The canoe rolled with the punches. By maneuvering carefully and using the engine we could run out from under breakers or slow to let others past. In a few minutes we were across the rough stretch and I steered into the calm channel, where Frank took over the paddling job. Horst was sure relieved.

The moose stood in the middle of the channel with their heads mostly underwater. They were busy feeding and didn't notice us. When we were 500 paces away from them Frank beached the canoe so we could approach on foot behind the screen of willows. The bull had small antlers, only about 40 inches, but they looked symmetrically grown. The cow was unmistakable -it had to be our old friend; she had the same butter-barrel belly and the same bell under her chin.

Horst had never killed a moose and was

understandably excited. We sneaked through the thick bush. When we were 300 paces from our quarry the bull seemed to have a notion that something was somehow not quite right in the landscape.

He looked in our direction.

Horst found a reasonably dry spot behind a bush and rested his rifle over a log. He readied himself to shoot and I nodded encouragement. I knew that his Remington 30-06 was sighted in at 250 paces and was certainly powerful enough to drop that moose.

"Just aim a little higher," I urged. He nodded.

The shot thundered out of the barrel. The bull flinched and I saw a small puff of water vapour escape from his left shoulder. A hard hit indeed.

Another shot whistled over the lake and blew the bull off his feet. Water splashed. The bullet had hit with a resounding smack. The cow had her head under water at the time and heard nothing of the shots. When she came up for air and saw the fallen bull she stood around until we approached with the canoe, then she scrambled for cover.

"What now?" asked Horst, "We can't dress him out here in the water?"

With a rope we tied the head and antlers to the outrigger bars to prevent undue drag and then we fired up the outboard motor. Thus we towed the floating moose back to camp where our mechanical winch lifted him high into a tree so we could skin and quarter him before supper.

We spent another three days enjoying the country before we packed up for the long drive home. One day Horst had the opportunity to bag a good caribou, but he let it go.

"What for?" he said. "We have enough meat now, and next year we'll be coming back — don't you think?"

"Of course we'll come back," I replied.

1980

Mountain sheep have always been the glamour game of B.C. hunters. Bread-and-butter-oriented hunters usually don't bother with sheep unless, of course, an exceptional opportunity presents itself. I have to confess that I have always been a keen student of the late Jack O'Connor, of Outdoor Life fame and although not a trophy hunter, I too appreciate great beauty wherever encountered.

Chapter 11:

Maybe Tomorrow

The rough-hewn shingles of the rotting cabin roof were hard underneath me as I lay and glassed the hillside above the rushing creek. The September landscape glowed green, gold and red, the blue-green of the spruce glistened and the leaves of the cotton willows and aspen shivered under an immensely blue sky. I had climbed onto the cabin roof to look over the tall brush that lined the ancient game trail that had lead me into this pass from my campsite at Surprise Lake, just east of Atlin. I was searching for a mountain caribou bull or a good bear trophy, but not for a mountain sheep.

Ever since the mid-1960's when I had killed a California bighorn ram in southern British Columbia I had bought sheep tag licenses - more out of patriotic duty than with serious intent to kill another ram — but on this far northern moose and caribou hunt I had no thought of sheep.

A fresh breeze blew through the mountain pass right into my face and made me duck behind the ridgepole of the cabin.

I spent an hour observing a pair of golden eagles soaring on an updraft to my right and began to daydream. I thought about my two partners who were fishing for grayling at the creek mouth. The fly-fishing was excellent and I looked forward to a delicious dinner. Suddenly a light coloured object I had thought was a rock moved swiftly, too fast for me to train the binoculars properly. Then it disappeared.

A timber wolf, was my first thought. I had seen an almost completely white wolf a few days earlier high up on a hillside considering that plenty of wolves roamed this mainly trackless country. I continued to search for another telltale movement, even though the freezing cold glasses jammed into my eye sockets threatened to give me a headache.

"He's gone. Too bad," I lamented. Then, just as suddenly, another white spot appeared in a stand of young blue spruce. It was apparently moving toward the trail and coming my way.

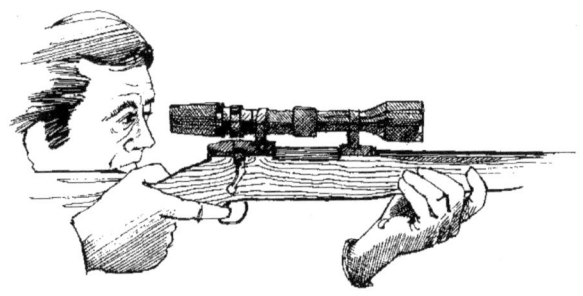

The distance between the spot and me was perhaps 400 yards, but I caught myself reasoning that the crystal-clear atmosphere of the north was probably playing tricks on my mind – like the time I spotted a large porcupine on a hillside a mile away and mistook it for a grizzly bear. The northern atmosphere does play such visual mirage tricks on hunters, which is probably why most tall tales come from the north. I mustn't make any mistakes this time, old boy, I told myself.

I checked my rifle. It was loaded and ready to use. From my prone position, resting the rifle on the ridgepole, I could risk a long shot if the animal would come into full view and stop for a moment. It was sighted in to hit the mark at 275 yards (a most sensible range for northern hunting). My 30-06 would shoot into an animal's vital area at 400 yards with an over-bold of about two feet. I was sure of this because I had target practised that kind of shooting on many occasions.

The white spot came closer and closer. Except for the movement I would have overlooked it completely. It stopped a few yards above the trail, and through the glasses I could see white body hair and a bluish-silver back. The animal took another step forward, turned and displayed its head, complete with great flaring amber-coloured horns —one magnificent stone ram. Then another ram pushed into view and both animals moved onto the trail towards me.

I put down the binoculars and slid behind the rifle. In front of me, less than 220 yards away, stood the most magnificent sheep I had ever seen in 28 years of hunting. The smaller ram had horns with a full curl, and the larger ram had horns that would easily go a quarter turn further in a beginning corkscrew.

My thumb flicked the Mauser's safety catch. I tried to suppress my excitement, to control my breathing — still the telescope's command post danced erratically over the ram's chest area. I almost fired. My finger had begun to squeeze the trigger when a most distressing thought crossed my mind. Where is my sheep tag? Do I have one? I recalled that I had purchased, as usual, a whole wad of game tags, but that in one location no sheep tag had been available.

The rams trotted slowly towards me. I fished my wallet out of my pocket to search for the tag. Silently I cursed the folks who had invented credit cards, purchase slips and all the other pieces of paper that cluttered up my wallet: my social insurance card, blood donor card, citizenship card, fishing license, steelhead license, and club membership cards.

If anyone had been watching they might have thought I was playing some kind of game without all the aces. Finally... my hunting license. With one eye on the rams I tried to read the categories that listed the number of tags I possessed. "Damn the fine print!" I cursed, "Where are my reading glasses?"

My breast pocket was empty. No glasses. I'd left them in the camp at Surprise Lake. In desperation I grabbed the binoculars, using them the wrong-way round like a magnifying glass. The line behind the word "sheep" was empty. I did not have a sheep tag and I am positive these sheep just knew it!

For over an hour the two rams grazed peacefully. Their snow-white necks and rumps glistening in the early morning sun, it was as though they were pure white and only wearing silvery-bluish-grey saddle blankets.

I must confess that some dishonest, unsporting thoughts came to mind. I no longer felt the rough shingles beneath me, as I started counting off on my shirt buttons, "Should I? Shouldn't I?" I was rudely interrupted in the middle of this when a wood sliver rammed into my hand. At that point the buttons came out in favour of "Shouldn't." I thought of my partners. What would they think and say if I suddenly showed up in camp with an untagged ram? I had no right to involve them in any illegal schemes. So "shouldn't" had won my little game.

"Be glad you saw a pair of good rams," I finally told myself. "There'll be another day, another year, another chance."

Reluctantly, but surprisingly much happier and calmer than I imagined I would be, I studied the great creatures until they vanished. Yes, I was certain there would be another year and a great reason to come back.

But two long years passed before I managed to return to the Atlin area. I persuaded a good friend to come with me.

"Sheep hunting? Here?" My partner had queried at first.

"Are you crazy? I'm still smarting from my car accident. I can't climb mountains and hike for umpteen miles just looking for a sheep. I thought we came for caribou."

"Don't worry about the climbing, "I said."I can't hike much either. I have a bad knee-cartilage problem. So any real climbing is out of the question. We'll just try something unorthodox." "Like what?" he asked skeptically.

"Like riding a trail bike to an old prospector's cabin and then sitting there until some rams show up," I said. "There is a cross trail. After the rams had gone I checked the area thoroughly— they use it to cross from one range to another. If we sit still long enough we'll get ourselves a sheep — I'm sure of it!"

"How long might that take?" he asked.

Of course I could not answer truthfully. "A day or two," I lied, "and if no sheep come past, we still have a chance at caribou, moose or grizzly bear. How about it?"

"I think you're crazy," was his grinning reply, "but I'm beginning to like the idea. When do you want to go?" "The middle of September." I replied.

"All right, mate, it's settled then." It was another cool clear morning when we packed our bikes and hobbled the last quarter mile to the sheep trail.

"Never seen one of these wild sheep," my partner confessed while trudging the trail up the last little rise and finally settling down behind a pair of huge boulders out of the stiff crosswind. "This better be good!" he proclaimed.

"Just sit still. Don't move around. Use your binoculars," I prescribed, "and keep anything that glistens or reflects the sun out of sight. Sheep are smart—very easily spooked — and they have exceptional eyesight."

The first hour of waiting was not too bad. Wearing forest green clothing we felt we could move our arms and legs a little bit without being spotted. My partner had set up his spotting telescope and was systematically searching the mountains for sheep. He didn't spot any and our wait became physically uncomfortable.

A small herd of caribou grazed on the hill above us within shooting range. Alas, the hunting regulations had unexpectedly been changed recently and we could not shoot the one beautiful bull in the herd.

"Let's have an early lunch," I suggested, attempting to prevent my restless friend from wandering about. If there is one thing I can do well, it is to sit still for long periods of time. Many years ago, I adopted the ambush-style of hunting that is widely practised in European countries, and have since learned since that I was at least as successful in my hunting efforts as most of my restless wandering friends.

Munching some cheese, bread and salami, I kept alert. I don't know why I happened to stare at a shale-covered spot on the mountains across the creek considering there was no logical cover there for a white sheep to hide. But strangely a tiny speck of white "rock" seemed to move.

The glass betrayed a flock of ewes and lambs. I aimed the spotting scope so my partner could finally see his first wild sheep.

"Hey, how did they get there?"

"I don't know," I replied, "my guess is they've been there all along."

In single file the sheep, seven of them,

moved around the base of the mountain and out of sight. For another hour my partner managed to sit still but then had to get up.

"I'm going over to look at the old cabin. I'm getting too stiff from sitting around." He was barely gone 10 minutes when I spotted a three-quarter curl ram on the hill on our side of the creek. Yeah, that ram had eyes only for my dear partner who failed to see the sheep, of course.

"We lost nothing," he stated later. "That three-quarter curl was not a legal ram anyway. We couldn't have taken him if we wanted to."

"True enough," I agreed, "but have you ever seen a single sheep anywhere? I mean without others close by?"

"Well, no."

"That's just the point. They almost never travel alone, and especially not the young rams. Chances are you stopped a bunch from crossing when you hobbled along the trail. Let's try again tomorrow, shall we? And no wandering about then or I'll come alone!"

That evening my friend took the opportunity to quiz a pair of experienced sheep hunters who shared the campsite with us. "Is it really true that sheep have exceptional eyesight? Don't they ever travel alone?"

"Yes and no," was the answer. "The only exception we ever saw was a real old ram that had only one horn. He was almost dead on his feet. We didn't shoot him. Who wants a poor looking trophy?"

"There is even a theory among some biologists that claims the old trophy sheep should not be hunted," the other hunter explained, "because being the recognized leaders in any flock, it is speculated by some folk that the younger rams don't become familiar with their home range and suffer high mortality rates because of it." (Me, I don't quite believe those theories but I know that the largest horns are usually out in front of the bunch.)

The following morning we were on the cabin trail early. As a precaution we left the bikes parked a considerable distance from the crossing. It was about 10:30 a.m. when I spotted the first of five sheep in the same area the ewes had been in the previous day. The 25X spotting scope was priceless now.

Soon we were at the cabin, watching the hillside. After an hour my companion was growing restless. Then, we spotted movement. At over 1,000 yards I could make out round circles of heavy horns. All were rams and feeding downhill towards the trail and our hiding place.

"Let's go get them," my partner whispered, after he had studied them for a minute.

"You'll never make it into shooting range," I commented. "Sit still. If not today, we'll get one tomorrow. We've got two weeks. Don't be impatient!"

As the rams came closer we could tell that they were all in the full-curl class.

"What if they don't come?" he asked. "Just be quiet!" I growled.

As if by magic, the rams arranged themselves in a single file and suddenly poured down the slope. They stopped occasionally and stared across, making us feel very self-conscious. On other mountains I had seen similar sheep behaviour. But despite our nervousness, on they came. At about 350 yards, on the bench above the creek, they stopped again. All were of legal size.

Then without warning, another ram popped out of the bush about 30 yards directly in front of us. My partner bounced to his supposedly aching feet and fired at him. The ram stopped momentarily as if stunned, and then proceeded toward a thicket of blue spruce as if nothing had happened.

I saw the flock across the creek making tracks fast-uphill, back to where they had come from. My partner made no effort to shoot again. He just stood there with his mouth open, apparently unable to believe that his ram might still get away. He was still travelling well, as if unhurt.

I fired just as the ram reached cover. We climbed down and hurried over to find him dead. My partner was the happiest hunter alive. It was his first sheep. With a grin as broad as a barn door he accepted my congratulations.

"We didn't do too badly for a pair of hobbling, battered up guys, did we now? Suppose you're going to tell me it was all planned, eh?"

"Well, wasn't it?"

"I think you were right this time. Reckon we can get one more for you?" he asked.

"Oh sure. Perhaps tomorrow maybe, or the day after. Or maybe next year. Wherever and whenever we find them. And don't forget to cancel your tag. You do have a tag?"

Of course, he did…

About the Author

Born in West Germany in 1929, Henry E. Prante apprenticed as a cabinet maker before moving to B.C. in 1952 and starting work as a boat builder. He opened his own boat works in 1967, Prante Boat Works Ltd., in order to provide for the family but also give himself more time for hunting and fishing. Having inherited a love for hunting from his grandfather, Henry lost no time exploring the province. From the Coast to the Rockies and north to the Yukon, he has hunted all the legal game species and brought home fresh meat for our family to eat. Nothing was wasted or killed for a thrill.

A dare and a friendly bet led to the start of his writing career in 1956 and by 1963 his first story was published in the Northwest Sportsman magazine. Running his own business and looking to the needs of his four children didn't leave much time for a formal education in English but by persevering and studying the works of such writers as Jack O'Connor, Jack London, Robert W. Service and Sir Winston Churchill, he progressed slowly but surely.

He also had a hunting adventure book published in Germany which sold out in short order (1986). This book also was a Canadian Bestseller and sold over 5,000 copies. Henry was a prolific writer and conservationist and there will be many more books to come after this one as soon as I can process them all.

Endnotes

Henry E. Prante passed away on February 27, 1992 at the age of 62 in Port Coquitlam from complications due to diabetes, strokes and heart disease. He is sadly missed by his family and other friends. Many of the hunting partners in this book have also met up with Dad in the Happy Hunting Grounds.

I hope you enjoy reading this book as much as Henry loved his many adventures as well, and then was able to re-live them by writing about them and share them with his partners and his readership.

As his daughter, I have a treasure trove legacy of all his adventures that will be published as fast as I can compile them and they will be published as separate volumes. Dad also was heavily invested in saving our local fisheries and in particular that Coquitlam River and its tributaries as well. I have the data he collected on this subject as well.

Please do sign up to the email list on the website so you can be notified when they are ready to be published in addition to other material I find that may be of interest to you amongst his personal papers and manuscripts, etc. I would also love to hear from you and I hope you will let me know how you enjoyed them.

Soon there will also be a collection of How-To Articles that were previously published in magazines as well. They will be listed on Amazon as an "in the Workshop" type series both in Kindle version and likely several per Print Book.

Henry also published this collection in German: Prante, Henry E: Kanadisches Jagdabenteuer — Dreißig Jahre im halbwilden Westen and it also sold out in short order. If I get enough interest I will republish it as well via eBook format and Print.

My Dad would have loved this new technology and would have made the most of it bringing you tales of his adventures. He can't anymore but I certainly will do my best to get his novel that is set in Atlin Lake BC, as well as other compilations of short stories. I am actually getting excited about going through these mountains of manuscripts.

Thank you.
Hella☺

A Few Photos:

Henry wished for a cabin like this ☺

Atlin October 1982

Taken by Sandy Lamberton

Atlin Wharf

Siesta time

Frank Apel and Dad's dog, Fritz ☺

Firewood Ferry

Dall Sheep Rams

Frank Apel

Frank Apel and Fritz

Henry

Town of Atlin

Atlin Lake

Atlin Hunting area

Teslin Lake Near Johnson Crossing

Surprise Lake (near Atlin BC)

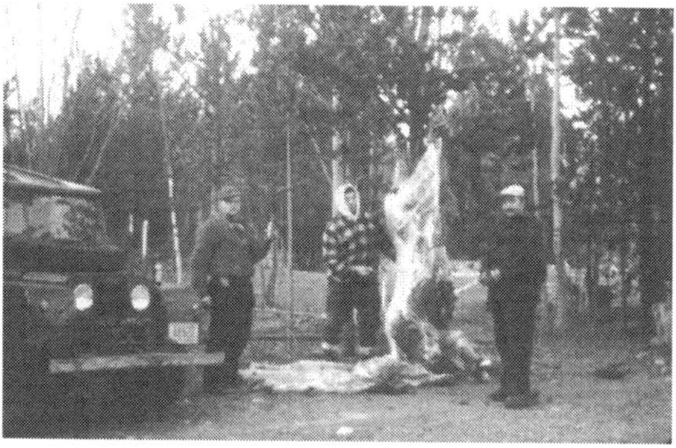

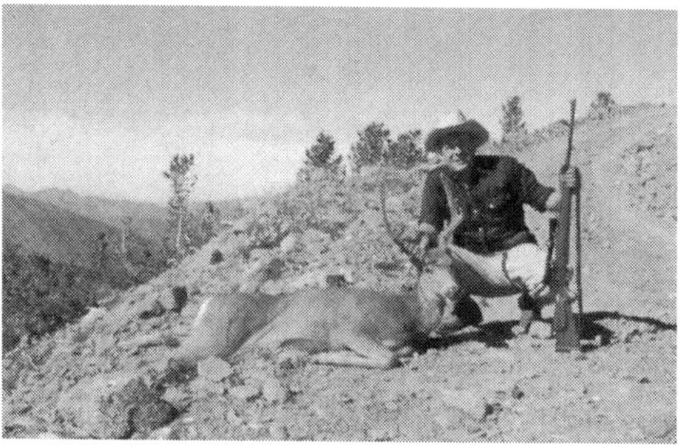

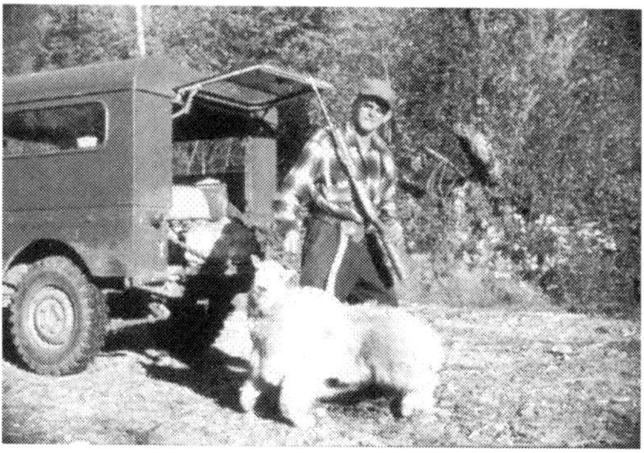

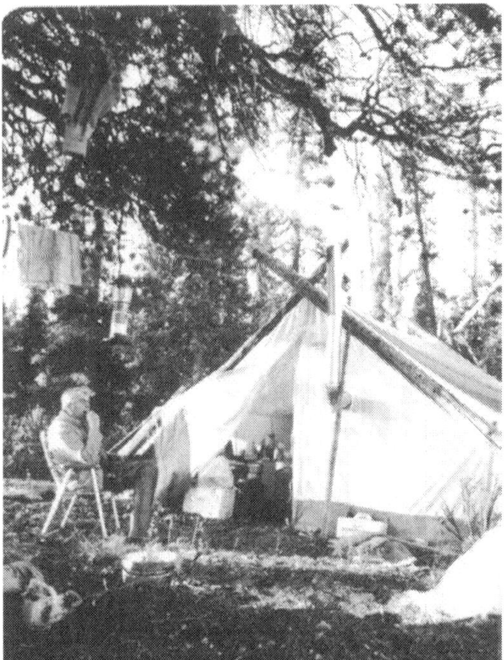

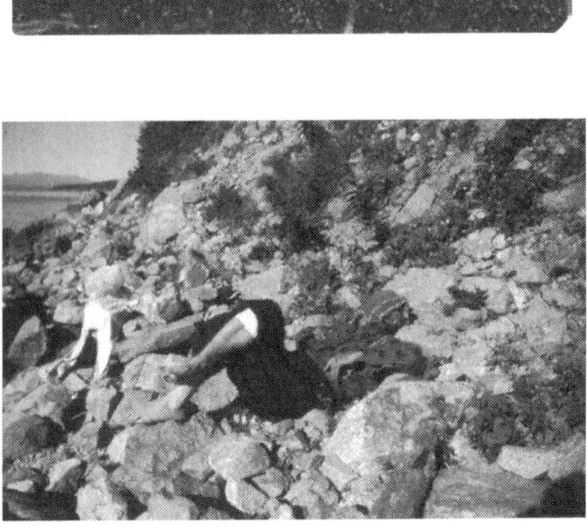

Henry and Frank Kasa

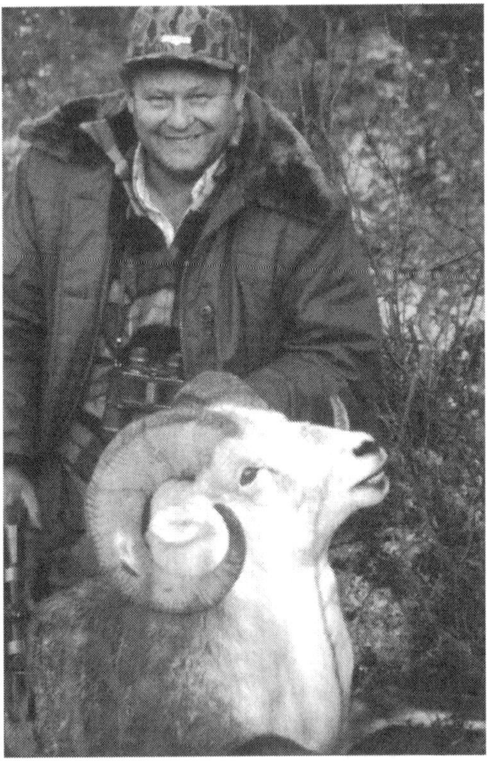

Horst Pothmann

Annabelle Apel

Henry's Good Dog, Fritz ☺

Henry Prante Sr. and his Bear

CONTACT ME:

I look forward to hearing from other hunters and outdoor enthusiasts and writers, as well— either through email or sign up to my email list on the website if you would like updates as I make them..

If you enjoyed this book then please leave a review on Amazon. It will go a long way towards getting this book seen by others like you. Thank you ☺

P.S. If you have a great hunting adventure that you want to have post on the website…drop me a line and let's see what we can do.

Hella Prante
Twitter @Hella_Chick
Hella@GreatHuntingAdventures.com

Made in the USA
Charleston, SC
04 April 2015